# PULPIT IN THE SHADOWS

By FREDDIE GAGE with STAN REDDING

PRENTICE-HALL, Inc., Englewood Cliffs, New Jersey

Dedicated to

THE REVEREND DAN VESTAL who led me to Christ

and

MR. RALPH P. GILBERT, Christian layman, who

has been a spiritual father to me and

the best friend a fellow ever had

and

To all the boys at TEEN LIBERATORS

# Foreword

This book is a fascinating story of an unfortunate boy who lived in the shadows and was completely throttled by sin. It is the story of how the redeeming power of Christ can lift one from the "shades of night" to spiritual victory. It is a story of spiritual liberation told by the person who was liberated.

Freddie Gage uses the language of the young people with whom he lived until the time of his new birth, and to whom he now ministers. The language and some of the story may be criticized by some, but this story of redemption is meant to bring hope to the unfortunate and misguided, and had to be told in their language to communicate. The author pulls back the curtain and lets us look at a raw, hard way of life that is as real as the mud puddle, the cloud or the hurricane. The story is well-done and holds out great hope for those in the grip of fleshly lust.

C. E. AUTREY
*Division of Evangelism*
*Home Mission Board*
*Southern Baptist Convention*

# Acknowledgments

I wish to acknowledge the following Christian men who have influenced my life:

Dr. J. Harold Smith
Dr. Jack Hyles
The Reverend Billy Graham
Dr. W. A. Criswell

I offer a special note of thanks to the dedicated Board Members of Teen Liberators:

The Reverend Don Berry
Judge Joe M. Guarino
Mr. Richard F. Pratt
Mr. C. W. Leisk
Mr. Paul Carlin
Lieutenant Breckenridge Porter
The Reverend Jarry Autrey
Dr. E. A. Driscoll
Mr. James E. Bird
Mr. Walter Rankin
Mr. Charlie Caspersen
Mr. Norman Norwood
Mr. Truitt Lively
The Reverend J. E. Barnwell
Mr. W. F. Conner
Mr. J .L. Rountree
Mr. Richard Huntoon

# Preface

Some men cannot compromise with convention. It is perhaps as well, for mankind, like bread, cannot rise without fer-
mentation. This is the story of one such man; a man who for
15 years has been the yeast in an unsavory dough of humanity.

Freddie Gage is an ordained minister of the gospel. But
there his link with religious convention is severed. In the
legions of the Lord, he is a rebel. In the staid hierarchy of
the ministry, he is a non-conformist. In the carefully thought-
out, polished oratory of the pulpit, his is the rash and dissi-
dent voice.

Before the Bar of Heaven, Freddie Gage is the "mouthpiece" for the hustler, the prostitute, the dope fiend, the
hood, the killer, the alcoholic, the scuffler, the restless and
the troubled. His story is of necessity—the story of those
who people the shadowy domain which society, properly or
improperly, terms the "underworld"—where Freddie Gage
has set up his pulpit.

The language herein, then, is in part the language of his
"congregation," the "hep" talk of the street gangs, the
"cool" tongue of the character. It has been expurgated only
to exclude the vilest of the words that lard the hoodlum's
vocabulary. Even so, there will be some who will be offended

v

# Preface

by this book and who will condemn it. There will be some ministers, perhaps, who will regard this book as unfit for a church library. Yet to tailor this story to the tastes of any one person or any one group would be to detract from its honesty and from the realities of life itself.

For the problems herein—sex, sin, corruption, juvenile delinquency, adult criminality, dope addiction, etc.—are not new problems. They are the same problems that confronted society when Jesus Christ walked this earth, the same problems that confronted society when His disciples walked this earth.

There is no intent herein to condemn the church as a whole, to reshape the church in its entirety, nor to censure any one minister or group of ministers.

The principal purpose within these pages is to awaken as large a segment of the ministry and lay church as is possible, to the realization that the problems posed herein *are the problems of the ministry and the church* and that the ministry and the church offers the principal solution to these problems—Jesus Christ, the Son of God.

STAN REDDING

# Language of the Trade

Every trade or profession has a language that is peculiarly its own. The diver speaks of the "bends," lawyers have words like "proxy" and "abstracts" and Christians speak of "being saved," of "conversion" and "rededication."

In the world of semidarkness where dope addiction thrives, they, too, have a language all their own.

So that you might better understand the subsequent pages of this book, I list words of their language and their meanings. They call it "jive language" and it is a rather weird vocabulary.

**bad go**—not enough dope for money paid
**bang**—an injection of heroin
**big kick**—to "get high," a "large charge"
**blast party**—teen-age get together for dope party
**boosted**—to steal something
**busted**—to be arrested
**cat, or hep cat**—narcotic user usually dressed "real sharp"
    hair combed in duck tail, talks jive language
**character**—one who uses dope
**cold turkey**—abrupt withdrawal for addicts

# Language of the Trade

**connection**—dealer in narcotics
**cover**—a "front" or business where drugs are sold, the selling of drugs being the main business
**deck**—paper containing heroin
**fix**—an injection of heroin
**get high**—smoking marijuana
**H.**—heroin
**hepster**—a character
**hide**—a girl
**hooked**—to become addicted to some form of drug
**hot shot**—an injection too powerful for one to live through
**hype**—an addict
**joy popper**—one who occasionally takes an injection
**junk or stuff**—meaning narcotics
**junkie**—an addict
**lusher**—one who prefers alcohol to narcotics
**M.**—morphine
**mainliner**—an injection directly into the veins
**monkey on his back**—one who has become an addict
**pad**—someone's house
**play it cool**—to keep one's wits
**pusher**—one who peddles dope
**reefers, weeds or sticks**—marijuana cigarettes
**red birds, yellow jackets**—barbiturates, sometimes referred to as "goof balls"
**score**—to purchase some type of narcotic
**square**—one who doesn't get high (on narcotics)
**stash**—money
**the "man"**—a detective
**yen**—a craving for narcotics
**bennies**—benzedrine pills
**blast**—to smoke marijuana
**clean**—an addict who is no longer using drugs
**snow, coke**—cocaine

# Contents

# Contents

# 1
# The Hepster

"IN THE MOUTH OF THE FOOLISH
IS A ROD OF PRIDE: BUT THE LIPS OF
THE WISE SHALL PRESERVE THEM."
—PROVERBS 14:3

T he detective was a gaunt and bony man with flaring ears and the doleful features of a tired foxhound. His name was as spare as his frame—B. Porter.

He tossed a switchblade on his desk and regarded me levelly with eyes that I knew could be gentle, but now were hard as fire opals. The shiv was mine, but I hadn't copped to it. Neither had Tommy, who sat picking his nails and ignoring the cop.

Detective Porter's voice rasped like coarse sandpaper on a rough surface. "You ain't tough, Freddie," he said, picking up the knife and regarding the dried blood on the haft. His thumb pressed down on the release button and the six-inch sliver of honed steel darted out like a rattler's tongue. "You're yellow, Freddie. Without this or a pair of knucks or a blackjack, you ain't got the guts to fight anyone your own size. None of you have!"

The detective raked Tommy with his contemptuous eyes. "I'll tell you something else, Freddie," Porter said. "You keep running with this tush hog and you won't live to be 21. This weedhead will put you in the chair, kid—don't you realize that? He's headed for the joint, boy, and he'll take you with him!"

Tommy's head snapped up and his sooty eyes glowed. I tensed, but Tommy didn't blow his cool. "Don't you worry about us, Mr. Porter," Tommy drawled with derisive politeness. "If we make it to the joint, we'll tell the warden you warned us. Okay?"

Porter's eyes grew bleaker. He opened the middle drawer of his desk and dropped the shiv inside. He laid his cold look on Tommy. "I'm not going to worry about you for one second, son," grated Porter. "You're dead, Tommy. You'll get into a beef with the wrong stud one day, and he'll shove a pistol in your belly and blow your gizzard through your backbone. Now get out of here, sprouts!"

We cut. Outside, Tommy looked back at the decrepit police station and spat savagely. He loosed a tirade of invective. "That skinny creep," Tommy choked. "I wouldn't need a shiv or a pair of knucks to take him! That lousy, crummy cop!"

I was a little put down myself. Porter had dropped me as a sprout and it rankled. I told myself I was tough, a real hood, but in the dark recesses of my mind, I wasn't so sure. I touched Tommy on the arm and said, "Cool it, man. Come on, let's go score for something." I started walking.

The feverish wildness in Tommy's eyes faded a bit as he fell into step beside me. Suddenly he laughed. "Did you hear what that fuzz said about me getting hit?" Tommy snorted. "Like hell! I'll be around when they close the lid on his coffin. That'll be a kick, man!"

But Tommy was wrong.

B. Porter was wrong, too.


If there's a Hell's Kitchen in Texas, it's on Houston's North Side.

There is no proven set of factors that will invariably

produce a criminal or a juvenile delinquent. There are neighborhoods with conditions more favorable to creating the criminal personality than others. The North Side, the "Bloody Fifth Ward," where I was born on April 1, 1933, is such an environment.

Many good people live on the North Side. They are decent, hard-working, law-abiding, church-going people. But there is a current of vicious lawlessness, an inculcated disregard for society and its mores, that swirls through the North Side, dominating its character; and the ebb and flow of that evil eddy shaped my life.

My father was a longshoreman on the Houston waterfront. He was a hard-fisted, hard-bellied man with tight, black curls, laughter-flecked eyes and a dockwalloper's boisterous ways. I worshipped my dad.

I also adored my mother, but my years with either of them were few. They were, in the language of the divorce courts, incompatible, and at the age of six, I became the offspring of a broken home. Mama took me and a new-born sister and went home to her parents. She didn't have far to go—my grandparents were North Side people, too.

They were among the North Side's good people. My grandmother was a woman of serene, unruffled bias, totally incapable of admitting any fault in her children or their children.

She welcomed my mother, my sister and myself into her house. And my grandmother showered a love on me in those years that was as blind and prejudiced as her faith in me was to be in future years. It was an adoration to which I was not accustomed—and one, I regret to say, I could not fully return.

My grandfather was a big, taciturn man, conservative in both actions and emotions. He rarely showed affection, even toward my grandmother; but he provided generously for all of us, and he never abused my sister or me. He did attempt to discipline me, but when he encountered vigorous opposition from my grandmother, he abandoned the issue and, except on rare occasions, treated me with aloof tolerance.

I was not happy in my grandparents' home. I felt squeezed in a cruel vise of insecurity and loneliness, and at night I wept with a silent longing. I felt unwanted by both my father and my mother, although such was not the case at all. I know now that both of them loved me.

Granddad owned and operated a café adjacent to a tavern on Humble Road, designated "Jensen Drive" on city maps and "U.S. 59 North" on state highway charts. Sheriff's deputies and police officers had yet another name for the narrow strip of asphalt that connected Houston with the lesser cities and towns in East Texas. They called it the "Bloody Burma Road" because of the violence that erupted nightly in the beer joints, pool halls, rooms-by-the-hour motels, dance halls and other raucous resorts that flank the neon-lighted highway.

Granddad catered to all comers—road-weary travelers, grimy-fisted roughnecks, squint-eyed truckers, horny-palmed laborers and an occasional sailor or cowhand—as did the tavern next door which Granddad didn't own. But the bulk of both the café's and the tavern's trade was neighborhood in nature, and some of Granddad's neighbors put quite a strain on the definition of the term.

Many of the people who draped themselves across the bar of the tavern or huddled around the tables in Granddad's café or sat in the booths were thieves, hoodlums, hustlers, junkies, safe burglars or some other caliber of crook. A few of them rated prominent mention in the Southwest's annals of crime.

But they dwelt in the vicinity. They were neighbors. Many of them also had children. Their children were my playmates and schoolmates.

The combination of social conditions and emotional forces

—blended together—proved a deadly mixture for me. My mother was the unwitting catalyst. She married again soon after her divorce from my father became final and left her parents to make a home with her new husband. She took my sister with her. She left me with my grandparents.

And with Baby Joe, who turned me out.

Baby Joe was my own age. He was a laughing, coal-haired child with the manners and mien of a cherub, all the instincts of a hungry leopard and a wisdom distilled from the wickedness of the ages.

Baby Joe was the "crown prince" of a dark empire. He lived with his family—including several uncles, aunts and cousins—five blocks away from my Granddad's café. The clan operated what was ostensibly an automobile salvage business, but in reality the sea of smashed cars masked a massive, statewide traffic in narcotics. Baby Joe's father was the titular head of the Texas dope domain and a major power in the nation's crime syndicate.

Baby Joe was well aware of his sacrosanct status and was tough and ruthless in asserting his standing. We attended the same elementary school, and from the third grade on, Baby Joe bossed his own gang—dubbed the Black Shirts.

I worked after school. I shined shoes, sold newspapers, ran errands and hustled popcorn and programs at area sporting events to earn nickels and dimes. But not Baby Joe.

He had his own "protection" racket going at school. Each school day scores of children handed over their lunch money to Baby Joe. This daily tribute bought them immunity from harassment and beatings at the hands of Baby Joe and his tiny terrorists. Baby Joe liked me and granted me an exemption from his lunch levy. He belittled my own earning efforts, however.

"Come in with me, kid, and I'll show you how to score," Baby Joe urged me. "Only squares scuffle for bread!"

7

His cajolery continued for months, but I resisted until my mother left me alone with my grandparents. I felt abandoned and, hurt and embittered, I promptly joined Baby Joe's band. Baby Joe was sympathetic and understanding.

"You can depend on me, kid," Baby Joe vowed. "I won't put you down!"

Baby Joe was an artful leader. I was soon his most ardent admirer and his staunchest follower. I copied Baby Joe's habits, mannerisms, speech and actions as closely as possible and defended him against any criticism. My adulation appealed to Baby Joe's warped ego. He made me his top lieutenant.

The gang's headquarters was a cluster of old bus and sedan bodies in the center of the several acres of wrecked vehicles behind Baby Joe's home. We converted the battered hulks into comfortable lairs, using the cushions, blankets, cots, stools, mattresses and other furnishings we acquired by devious methods.

A select few of the Black Shirts, myself included, were also allowed to visit in Baby Joe's home, which was frequented by many notorious outlaws and gangland overlords who congregated there to gamble, drink or discuss illicit operations. I was impressed and awed by these "big time operators," who always drove flashy cars and sported large bankrolls.

They also had a lofty disdain for the lesser criminals whom they used to their own advantage, but to whom they accorded no social standing whatever.

I made up my mind that I'd be a big time operator.

In the jargon of the underworld, we kids were "sprouts." Sprouts generally live their own lives, without discipline or restraint—and a minimum of advice—from their elders in crime. Baby Joe's band, like all kid gangs, made the most of this lack of restriction. We played hooky from school, we stole, we took part in "rumbles" or fights with other gangs

8

and we engaged in all sorts of malicious mischief—slashing automobile tires and convertible tops, pouring sand and salt into gasoline tanks, smashing plate glass store windows and ravaging classrooms.

Ours was a calculated criminality, our depredations planned and executed deliberately and often without reason. I had no sense of wrongdoing, so skillfully had I been indoctrinated, and only an occasional twinge of conscience.

Actually, for the first time in my life I felt I belonged—that I was somebody! Such is the psychological appeal of the gang for kids unloved and unwanted at home, or kids who *feel* they are unloved and unwanted at home.

You grow up fast in a street gang. By the time I was 13, I knew things the birds and the bees didn't know. I packed a shiv and a pair of brass knucks, I hated cops and school officials, I was contemptuous of "squares" and I wore tailor-made "drapes," an affectation I felt would aid in dispelling any notion that I was a sprout.

The first time I showed up at the Queen in a silk shirt, pegged pants, $35.00 cardigan and $30.00 alligator shoes, someone whistled and exclaimed: "Man, dig Freddie *The Cat!*" The name stuck. I became The Cat.

The Queen was a theater, the unofficial "union hall" of the North Side gang members—the place where they met to plan a caper, discuss their latest scores, get up a rumble or settle a beef. Whatever motion picture was showing was secondary.

A strict caste system prevailed at the Queen. The older hoods and toughs—some of whom were "way out cats" who sported earrings—sat in the balcony. Sprouts were relegated to the first floor, with the exception of Baby Joe. He had a seat in the balcony.

I was introduced to marijuana—also known as "weed," "grass," "tea," "hemp," "pot" and "reefers"—at the Queen. Most of the balcony crowd smoked pot, but there was a strict ban on smoking the weed downstairs. It was too easy for the cops to sneak up on you there. The sprouts compensated by smuggling in "lush"—beer, wine or whiskey—in paper cups or soft drink bottles and getting bombed on the booze. I did it myself, but what I really wanted was to join the balcony crowd. I racked my brain for a way to join that exalted throng.

In the end it was muscle, not mentality, that bought me a ticket to the balcony.

A bunch of us were cutting up downstairs one Saturday afternoon. There was a new usher, a "square John," working the lower floor. He was tall, with a football player's shoulders, and it was obvious that he didn't know what kind of people frequented the Queen. He grabbed me when I went to the restroom.

"Look, kid, one more ruckus down front and you're all going out," he said in a determined voice.

I slid my hand in my pocket while he talked and worked my knucks on over my fingers. Then I copped a "Sunday" on him. I hit him in the jaw with a right hook and he dropped like he had been poleaxed. I started kicking him and then, in a frenzy, knelt astraddle of him and began hammering at his head and face with my brass-bound fist. The manager and several others pulled me off the guy, and the manager threw me bodily into the street. I looked down at the blood all over my shirt and slacks, and the sight of the gore scared me. I cut out, fast. I figured I had killed the usher.

I had hurt him badly. But no one would tell the cops who had assaulted him, and the manager wasn't sure himself, because of the dimness of the interior, who the attacker was. I stayed away until the heat cooled and then returned one Saturday. I walked boldly up the stairs to the balcony and to the row where Baby Joe was sitting.

10

# The Hepster

I stood there in the aisle, challenging the older toughs with my presence. Several of them stared at me coolly.

Then a voice drawled from behind me, "Sit down, Cat, you're blocking the view." I eased down beside Baby Joe, who grinned and playfully poked an elbow into my ribs. I was in.

All around me, kids were blasting pot. Marijuana has an odd odor, something like rope burning. Maybe that's why it's sometimes called hemp.

After a few minutes, Baby Joe murmured, "Want to get high?"

I was both tempted and scared. "I don't want to get hooked," I finally hedged.

Baby Joe laughed softly. "Man, it ain't as bad as that old lush. That'll make a wino out of you. This grass is really kicks." He lit a stick and placed it between my lips. "Here. Draw in deep and hold the smoke down inside you. Get a kick, Cat, get a kick!"

I wasted half the slim cylinder before I got the knack of it, but it was kicks! First I felt dreamy and then there was a tremendous sense of exhilaration. I seemed to grow until I filled the theater! I felt big, important, full of power! I was really loaded.

Marijuana isn't really addictive, no more so than cigarettes. But it's a dangerous narcotic, for it plays false tricks on the mind and does away with inhibitions and sane reasoning.

In addition, sooner or later the kicks from grass grow stale and the user turns to "joy-popping"—the occasional use of heroin—for a bigger boot. From "joy-popping" to the regular use of "H" is just one more easy step. Tinker to Evers to Chance—and you're hooked on a barb forged in hell.

But that day I thought grass was the greatest!

## Pulpit in the Shadows

My prestige went up like General Motors after I crashed the balcony set at the Queen, but I knew I was still just a 13-year-old sprout in the eyes of the older Black Shirts. A guy never really arrives in a gang until he makes out with one of the older "Mollies."

"Mollies" are girls, also called "debs," "dolls," "babes," "broads" and "chicks." Gang girls. Every gang has its female auxiliary, for delinquency has always been a coeducational institute. Girls contribute a lot to a gang, but mostly they contribute sex, a principal pastime of street packs.

Our girls ranged in age from 13 to 16, and they all shared their sexual favors indiscriminately with the male members of the gang—all except five teen-age girls recruited by Pico, a member of the Black Shirts who had definite ambitions. Pico had aspirations of one day heading up a ring of call girls, and he figured he might as well get in some practice while he was young. Like all pimps—would-be or active— Pico was suave, charming and attractive to women. His five girls were devoted to him, and if you wanted to play with one of his girls, you paid a half-dollar to Pico for the pleasure.

I went for girls. My sexual experiences, however, had been confined to peep shows and to the vicarious pleasures derived from the pornographic pamphlets, pictures and "comics" that circulated freely among the sprouts. I had refrained as much from shyness as from any other reason.

After I started smoking weed, I lost my shyness.

I also lost interest in the gang's petty activities. I felt it was senseless to steal nickels and dimes. "Look, if we're going to get caught, man, let's make it for something right!" I protested to Baby Joe one night. "Let's score big!"

Baby Joe nodded. "You're right, Cat. It's time we quit being junior jivers." Sprouts were sometimes called "junior jivers."

12

## The Hepster

We picked an ice house as our first major mark. An ice house in Texas is a pretty lucrative business because most of them also deal in beer, wine, groceries and drug items.

There were five of us in on the job. My share of the swag was $65.00. "Man, we're going to make a lot of bread from now on," exalted Peg, so-called because of his gimpy walk.

We did, too. We burglarized stores, laundromats, service stations, hardware stores and other business places for cash and merchandise. We looted swank apartments and plush residences of valuable furs, clothing, appliances and jewelry. We split the cash and fenced the merchandise. Usually, not more than five or six members of the gang took part in any one given caper, but Baby Joe, Peg, a kid named Spanky and myself were almost always in on any score.

Crime paid good for me. I was 13, and I was knocking down $100 a week and more!

We were operating out of our league, of course. But no one said anything. As long as we weren't stepping on any toes, no one put up a beef. Our adult mentors, in fact, were proud of us. Only once did we come close to overstepping ourselves.

Baby Joe and I decided to knock over a jewelry store. It was a branch store of a national chain, and it had no place on the North Side, really. But there it was, glistening new, offering real diamonds, pearls, emeralds and gold to the working stiffs for so much down and so much a month. Baby Joe and I coveted the glittering treasures in the store, but the only down payment we had in mind was a brick.

We were casing the joint for about the third time when Baby Joe nudged me and nodded toward a man talking to a salesman up front. I recognized him at once. Jug Silvers, a real tough outlaw. Silvers and his cronies were real safemen and gunmen, and you didn't mess with them unless you had a stomach strong enough to digest pure lead.

13

Silvers had seen us. He finished his conversation with the clerk and strolled over to the showcase where we were standing. He lit a cigarette and let his eyes wash over us. They were cold and blue, the eerie blue of St. Elmo's fire.

"Flee the scene, sprouts," he murmured and walked on toward the rear of the store. We got the message.

A few days later, Baby Joe dropped a newspaper in my lap. The headline on the front page told the whole story: NORTH SIDE JEWELRY STORE ROBBED OF $7,500 IN CASH AND GEMS!

The fact that Silvers had pulled a "freeze out" on us didn't bother us a bit. We had a new gimmick, one that was proving profitable. On nights when we weren't knocking over some business firm, we'd follow a bus to some lonely section of the city. When a passenger got off who looked like he might have a few bucks on him, we'd swing into action.

One of us would intercept the man as he left the bus stop and halt him on the pretense of bumming a match or asking directions. Another of us—usually me or Spanky—would slip up behind him and slug him with a sap. Then we'd roll the guy and cut out. We fractured a few skulls that way, according to the newspapers.

We made our biggest score that way, too, and lost both it and Spanky. One night, we slugged an old man, and he had $600 on him! One of us always took all of the loot on this type of caper, then we'd go our separate ways and meet next day to divide the take. That way, if any of us were ever picked up by the cops, only the one with the loot had any worries.

The next day after we scored for the $600, Spanky walked over to a bus stop to catch a bus to Baby Joe's home. He was standing there, not paying any attention to what was going on around him, when people started screaming and vacating the vicinity. Spanky looked up then, but it was too

14

late. A cement truck, fully loaded, had sideswiped a car and the driver had lost control. The cement truck careened across the street, turning over en route, and when Spanky first saw it, it was coming down on top of him.

The cops who investigated the accident found the six C-notes on his body. Naturally, they were interested in learning where a 14-year-old kid, son of a convict and a $30-a-week waitress, had acquired $600. They connected it up right away with the old man who had been robbed the night before and then started questioning Spanky's friends, me and Baby Joe among them. That's how I first met B. Porter.

We were picked up by juvenile officers, but Detective Porter talked to all of us, since the homicide squad handles rapes, robberies, murders and other violent crimes. He was a gentle man, and I was contemptuous of him at first. I put him down as a "softie."

I denied any knowledge of the robbery. I said I knew Spanky, but only slightly, since I didn't even attend the same school. I didn't fool Porter, but he let me think I had because he knew I wasn't going to tell him anything. He switched to talking about school and sports and what I wanted to be when I grew up. And then he asked me, casually: "What church do you attend, son?"

"Church!" I exclaimed, startled. I had never been to church. My soul existed on the same lean rations as my heart and mind. "God," in my tumultuous little world, was part of an angry word. "Jesus Christ" was an exclamation. I laughed. "I don't go to no church, mister. What could a church do for me?"

Detective Porter smiled and stood up. He dropped a hand on my shoulder and squeezed, and I knew suddenly that this cop was tough—that as slender and harmless as he looked, he'd handle Jug Silvers easily. "You might be surprised," he said cheerfully and left me.

15

I told Baby Joe about Porter's remark. Baby Joe doubled up with laughter. "That's what you need, Cat! Some of that old-time religion!" Baby Joe howled gleefully.

It broke me up, too. Me—go to church! I was Baby Joe's right hand—Freddie the Cat, the roughest of the Black Shirts. That would really be kicks, man—me in church!

But that night, as I had many nights before, I woke up to find myself crying. And I asked myself a question: If I was so rough and tough, why did I cry?

16

# 2
# The Cat Takes Command

"HE WHO IS BENT ON DOING EVIL
CAN NEVER WANT OCCASION."
—PUBLILIUS SYRUS, 42 B.C.

I got up mad at my dad.

It was a bitterness born of want. I hadn't seen my father in several months. I hadn't even talked to him on the telephone.

Dad didn't like to come to my grandparents' home. They resented his presence in their house for any length of time whatever. Sometimes, when he came to visit me, their animosity was almost tangible.

I knew the score. But I felt Dad could at least phone me—maybe have me meet him somewhere else—and when he didn't, I began to build up an enmity for him myself.

I was still brooding over my father's inattention when I walked into the malt shop near the junior high school in which I had just enrolled. The malt shop, for many reasons, was the most popular hangout for neighborhood teen-agers.

Baby Joe and several Black Shirts were there, cutting up the jackpot (talking) with some dolls. A few square sprouts were feeding the juke; and back in one corner, sprawled indolently in their chairs, were Duck and Bruce.

They were about 20, these two, and as alike as wolf cubs from the same litter: black hair, mahogany skin, high cheeks, eyes like chips of carbon.

Duck and Bruce weren't students. They were dope pushers.

I dropped into a chair across from them and nodded. They knew me, but they had never sold me any stuff. They looked at me guardedly. "What you want, Cat?" Bruce finally asked.

I turned my hand and showed the $5.00 bill folded in my palm. "Weed," I said softly. "You got the grass—I got the bread." Duck lifted the coke in front of him, took a swig and started to say something.

But Baby Joe caught his eye and nodded. Then Duck relaxed. "How many sticks?" he asked.

I dropped the fin on him. "All of it. Ten sticks." Bruce nodded. A few minutes later, he stood up and stepped to the counter where the candy bars, cookies, peanuts and other snacks were displayed. When he came back, he dropped a bag of corn chips in front of me.

"Here, man, you look hungry," he remarked casually.

I had just connected. I stay loaded all day on that sack of "chips."

Of all the phantom areas composing the legendary underworld, none is so nebulous as that peopled by the dealers in narcotics. They are the most despicable criminals, abhorred even by many segments of their own lawless society.

The murderer takes only a life; the rapist violates only the body; the thief and the bandit, after all, take nothing that cannot be replaced. But the dope dealer enslaves the body and soul. He robs the mind of reason and the heart of hope. He condemns men and women—and their dreams, ambitions and capabilities—to a living death. His crime cannot be measured individually, for the effects of dope radiate outward, and its fallout of despair and degradation touch the lives of those far removed from its evil explosion.

The dope dealer prizes anonymity. He covers his trail as skillfully as any Sioux horse thief ever brushed out his pony tracks. The real dope dealers are never addicts themselves.

They know too well the ways in which marijuana, heroin and other drugs can crush the spirit and maim the mind.

Dope dealers may use addicts as pushers in areas where there is danger of detection. They even use addicts as smugglers or connections, but they are never known to the addicts. A junkie has no secrets when the monkey on his back is screaming.

For a dope dealer, Duck and Bruce were the ideal henchmen. They weren't addicts. They were tough and wouldn't crack under pressure if caught. And they were ruthless enough to take any steps necessary to protect themselves and their source—if, indeed, they knew for whom they worked—from disclosure.

Duck and Bruce were also the lowest of their breed. They peddled dope to school children.

When I made my second buy from them, I got down on their level.

"You ain't no fink, Cat," Duck remarked casually. "You wouldn't finger us to the Man."

I bristled. "Who said I would, anyway? I'm no punk! What kind of rib are you guys putting down?"

Bruce raised his hand. "Take it easy, kid. It's no rib. We just figured you might like your grass free. How'd you like to get some other people turned out?"

I snapped at the chance—I didn't even hesitate. "Yeah, why not?" I agreed.

As easy as that, I hit bottom. I became a junior high school "leader," touting my schoolmates on the pleasures of marijuana!

I put a lot of them on it—Donnie, Troy, Sparrow, Jughead, Little Red and many others whose names are branded on my conscience. I wish it weren't so, but a lot of those kids went from hemp to heroin, became hooked and, like all junkies, were driven to the extremes of crime to finance their hellish hunger for drugs.

At the time, however, I considered myself a real sharpie. I

21

used the extra sticks of weed I earned to enhance my power in the gang. I threw a lot of "tea parties," and while none of the parties made the society pages, some of the "guests" later made the police blotter.

Shortly after I became a shill for Duck and Bruce, I glanced at the headline of a newspaper and then grabbed it from the rack. Baby Joe's uncle—one of my idols—had been killed in a gunfight with a Texas Ranger. He and a notorious safe burglar had been surprised by the Ranger while robbing the safe of an East End department store. The other hood had been badly wounded in the midnight shoot-out.

That same afternoon, Baby Joe sought me out. "The whole family's hot," he said tersely. "We're cutting out for Louisiana, and I don't know when I'll come back. The gang is all yours, Cat—all yours!"

I walked around for several hours, giddy with authority. I had exactly 100 tough kids who would take my orders!

The Black Shirts quickly learned that I was an able gang leader. Under me, activity stepped up—we hit dozens of business places and apartments.

I shared in the loot whether or not I was an active participant in a particular caper. When any member of the gang ventured to protest, I worked him over with brass knucks or a slapjack.

"You're hard, Cat—harder than a loan shark's heart," Little Red grunted after one such incident. It was a compliment.

Those were hectic times for me, marked by senseless and savage violence, sex orgies, dope parties, drinking sprees and other forms of debauchery. I was high on weed a lot of the time, as were a lot of my companions, and the grass governed our behavior to a large extent. We'd pile into cars late at night and drive to The Courts, a low-rent government apartment complex, and lure as many girls from their pads as possible for sex parties that might last until dawn. We'd steal cars, drive to Galveston, and blow all the proceeds of a lucrative job in the Island City's bawdy houses. We were continually prowling the city's and county's nightclubs, taverns and dance halls in search of excitement.

When we couldn't find any excitement, we made our own. There was a teen-age dance in Kashmere Gardens, which we referred to scornfully as "Podunk." Some of us crashed the party. We weren't only loaded on pot, we had also been eating "redbirds" and "yellow-jackets," which are barbiturates. The Podunk boys didn't welcome our making the scene all pilled up and loaded, but they let it ride. They didn't want a beef.

But *we* did. I started pranking around with their gang leader's doll and dropping them as squares, knowing he'd have to brace me. He did, eyes smoldering.

"Man, you better snap," he warned me. "You're not going to run this end of town."

I racked him back with a right hook. He grabbed a chair and swung it, and I cut him. My shiv sliced through his jacket and shirt and ripped his back open. A girl screamed, and a wild melee erupted.

We were outnumbered, so we fled. The Kashmere Gardens gang leader was taken to the hospital, but he refused to tell the cops who had cut him. He sent word on the grapevine that his gang would settle for him.

The rumble was set for that night, near a Podunk drive-in theater. I took 30 Black Shirts to the scene of combat and found 60 Podunkers waiting. We piled out of our cars. "Let's get 'em," I rapped, and led the Gang toward the rival gang group.

One of the Kashmere Gardens gang members suddenly opened up with a revolver. The Black Shirts halted and began to mill, on the verge of panic. Guns had never figured in any of our fights until then.

I noticed the kid with the pistol was triggering his loads into the air. "Come on," I shouted. "He ain't got the guts to shoot anybody." We plunged into the rival ranks, swinging short lengths of chain, lead-weighted sticks, beer bottles and brass-encased fists.

We smashed the Kashmere Gardens gang quickly and were gone before police, summoned by the theater manager, arrived.

The cops began leaning on us. Within a period of two months, 25 or 30 Black Shirts were convicted in juvenile court on a variety of charges and committed to the state reform school for juvenile boys. Any one of them could have beat the rap by putting the finger on me. The cops wanted me badly.

"We've got a tag on you, boy," one particularly tenacious policeman told me. "We'll bust you, somehow or someway."

"Why?" I protested with a feigned show of innocence. "I ain't done nothin'."

The cop's lips curled in a disdainful smile. "Like hell you haven't."

The police began bugging my grandparents. They didn't really want to send me to the reform school, the cops told them. They'd rather see me straightened out. They urged my grandparents to exercise stricter control over my associates, actions, activities and hours. My grandfather listened with a sour smile. My grandmother reacted in typical fashion—she denounced the officers.

"Freddie's never done anything wrong," she finished angrily. "He's just been in with a bunch of bad boys, and doesn't realize they're bad boys, that's all!"

One policeman exploded. "Granny—*he* is a bad boy! He's the leader of that bunch of bad boys! This kid is using narcotics! Can't you understand?"

My grandmother couldn't understand. She never did understand.

It seems incredible that she didn't. I had a dozen pairs of

expensive shoes under my bed. My closets were stuffed with tailor-made suits, slacks and sport coats, all of the finest material. My bureau drawers were crammed with expensive shirts, underwear, socks, sweaters and other luxurious accessories. I always had bread on me. My grandmother was well versed in North Side economics. It should have been painfully clear to her that a 15-year-old couldn't maintain such a wardrobe and sport such personal wealth on the income from a shine box, a newspaper route and odd jobs. But it wasn't clear—ever.

School officials were more perceptive. They were certain any "odd jobs" I performed were burglaries, robberies and thefts. You can't be a successful juvenile delinquent and an A-student, too. School bored me. I was a chronic truant. When I attended classes, I left my books in my locker. I never did any homework. Consequently, I spent most of my time at school in the principal's office, being reprimanded or lectured.

Many of my teachers and principals made genuine efforts to divert me from my wayward course. Most of them spent hours of their own time counseling me, interceding for me, doing whatever else they could do to avert my seeming self-destruction in the quicksands of crime.

I didn't listen to them. I didn't appreciate their efforts. They could do nothing with me. They held out to me that which I yearned for more than anything else—affection, trust and respect—and I was unmindful of the offering.

I walked out of a classroom one day and a juvenile officer grabbed me. "Come on, you're going to reform school this time," he snapped.

He marched me through the halls, outside, and down the sidewalk to his car. We passed hundreds of gaping students and, aware of the stir I was causing, I put a swagger in my walk and affected a cocky smile. I felt as though I'd really arrived, being busted in front of the whole school!

I felt less honored when I was booked into the juvenile

detention ward in old Jefferson Davis Hospital on a nebulous charge of "habitual delinquency." Oscar Wilde could have written another ballad about that vile and filthy jail for children. It was a stench in the nostrils of humanity.

The place was alive with lice and bedbugs. The plumbing was faulty and the odor of urine and excrement permeated the atmosphere, inducing nausea. Lewd poems and comments were scribbled all over the dirty plaster walls, and homosexuality was rampant in the "tanks" where the young prisoners were held. In later years, indignant judges, probation department officials and newspapermen succeeded in abolishing the hell-hole, and it was replaced with one of the cleanest, most modern juvenile facilities in the nation.

I lay in the dungeon-like lockup and my hatred toward society solidified.

Juvenile officers questioned me. They didn't really have anything definite that they could pin on me. They suspected that I was behind a mint of burglaries that were still unsolved on their books, and they were right—but I wasn't about to confess.

One juvenile officer, a lanky lieutenant with saturnine features and a musing voice, seemed more concerned about my future deeds than my past activities. "You've got the ability to make something good of yourself, lad," he advised me. I laughed at him.

"Sure! Everybody tells me to be good, but nobody tells me how to be good. Tell me!" I challenged him.

"You know how," the lieutenant replied quietly. "Quit stealing, quit smoking that weed, quit lying. Go to school, and get an honest job. It's that simple and you know it."

Maybe I did, but I wouldn't admit it.

When my day in court came, the juvenile judge paroled me to my father. "In other hands, this boy has been incorrigible," the judge told Dad. "Perhaps you can do something with him."

Dad didn't know how.

# The Cat Takes Command

I had always used the cars of other Black Shirt members, or stolen one, when I needed a car; but suddenly I decided I wanted a real sharp set of wheels of my own. I conned my Dad into letting me buy one. "I really need one for school," I pleaded.

I had become a school gypsy. I had been expelled from the one junior high school on my arrest. My stepmother enrolled me in another when I moved into her home. I lasted only a few weeks. A pocket-sized blonde caught my eye the third week. "Who's the stacked-up chick?" I asked Little Red, one of the many Black Shirts who also attended the school. Little Red grinned.

"That's Lois," he said. "She's a preacher's daughter. She goes with some high school football player who's supposed to be tough."

I arranged to be introduced to Lois that afternoon. I put down a good line, and she slipped out of her house that night and met me.

We went to a drive-in movie. Little Red and his girlfriend were with us. Not 30 minutes later Lois' boyfriend showed up and parked near us. Lois was a little nervous until she saw her boyfriend had another girl with him—then she became angry.

It was strictly for Lois' benefit that Little Red and I began putting the guy down. I told him I had his girl, and I told him what I was going to do to her. He took it as long as he could, then walked over to our car. I got out, as did Little Red, but the girls stayed in the car. The guy—I learned his name was Ronnie—leaned down to speak to Lois. "What's going on?" he asked. Before she could answer, I pulled Ronnie around.

"Go away, man," I snarled. "If you don't, I'm going to cut your head off!"

Ronnie's face tightened. "I won't fight you, Cat. You won't fight fair, and I don't know how to fight dirty."

He was right. I didn't know how to fight fair. I slugged

him with a coke bottle; and when he hit the ground, I began to kick him. Little Red pulled me off. I laughed and got back into the car. "You're mine now, baby," I told Lois. She was big-eyed with adoration. I dropped her the next day.

The school dropped me, too, after Little Red and I led the Black Shirts in a rumble with a rival gang right on the campus!

I enrolled in a school in Galena Park, a small city on the Houston Ship Channel. The big-man-on-campus had heard of me, and he sought me out the first day. "I'm called Claudie Boy, the Cat," he grinned. "But I guess it'll just be Claudie Boy while you're here."

He had a convertible, a real sharp heap. That afternoon he rounded up two sexy dolls, I scored for some weed and the four of us drove to a secluded section of the country and got loaded.

I didn't last long at the school. I was expelled as a bad influence on the student body.

My stepmother wasn't happy with me. She was a good woman, a Sunday morning church-goer, and she bugged me about my activities, my hours and my friends. "If you weren't ashamed of your friends, you'd bring them home to visit," she pointed out.

So I did. I began bringing home dope users, teen-age prostitutes and hoods—much to my stepmother's horror. She didn't inquire into my comings and goings too much after several such visitations.

My life was a frenetic carrousel of crime, carnality and corruption. The top echelon of the Black Shirts were no longer junior jivers. Some of us were teaming with hardened adults, many of them ex-convicts, to pull burglaries and robberies.

I was restless for new thrills, frantic for new kicks.

I had put Bucky on weed. Then he put me on heroin. I was at a club one night and walked into the restroom to find

Bucky, Troy and Rip "fixing." Bucky had a spoon into which he had poured heroin. He mixed the powder with water, heated it with a match held under the bowl of the spoon and drew the warm liquid into a hypodermic syringe. He then injected the narcotic into the vein of his left wrist. "We ain't hooked, we're just chippin'," he grinned at me. "Want to fix?"

I didn't. I was well aware of the dangers of heroin. You could "chip" or "joy-pop" once a week or once every two weeks and not get addicted to the stuff, but few people can really just chip with "Horse." Usually, they began joy-popping two or three times a week, then once a day, and then one morning they wake up with a 40-pound monkey on their back.

"Not me," I said, throwing up my hands. Bucky scowled. "Hey, man—you told me how good weed was, and I tried it. Now, I'm telling you how good this stuff is, and you're chicken if you don't try it."

I let them rib me into it. Bucky mixed a paper of heroin and injected it into a vein of my left arm.

The effect on me was typical of the narcotic. I was hit with a "flash," that is, I became sick and vomited. Then the nausea passed, replaced by an intense euphoric sensation. I felt like I had blasted 50 sticks of weed!

I chipped with "H" for about six months. During that period Rip, Donnie and Troy all became hooked, although they ribbed themselves that they weren't. I got most of my dope free because I took a lot of boys to Duck and Bruce to connect for hemp and heroin. They both knew I was chipping around with heroin. They didn't say anything, but I saw a mocking contempt in their eyes.

One morning I woke up with a "yen" for a fix. "Man, you better pull up and quit," I warned my reflection in the mirror. For the first time in my life, I took the advice offered me. Maybe because it was my own. The next time Bruce

slipped me a capsule of heroin, I slipped it back. "Keep it,"
I said firmly. "I'm off the stuff."

Bruce nodded. "Smart boy," he murmured wryly.

I began running with pimps. I had decided I'd someday
have a stable of play-for-pay fillies; and, like Pico, I felt a
bit of early practice wouldn't hurt. Running a call girl ring, I
reasoned, would be less chancy and far more lucrative than
blowing boxes or holding up supermarkets. I didn't think I'd
have any trouble recruiting girls—I egotistically told myself
that I was attractive to girls and could bend almost any
chick to my will.

One night Pico, myself and several other older Black
Shirts dropped into a combination roller skating rink and
beer hall. It was a favorite haunt of hoodlums and gang
girls, and was frequented in large numbers by square babes
and "half-hep" chicks on the make. We were just cruising.

A young boy slouched against a post, sipping a beer and
watching the girls. He was in my way and I hipped him.
"Move!" I said curtly. He moved, like an angry rattler. He
sprang sideways and lit on the balls of his feet, facing us. He
was as wiry as steel wool, with flat-planed cheeks and a
finely-arched nose. He had even, white teeth, displayed in a
snarl of anger, and his eyes were dark wells of hate.

He threw his beer on my shoes and spat in the puddle.
"Don't ever touch Tommy again," he hissed. "You junior
jiver! You're all junior jivers—I'll take on all of you."

I knew him when he spoke his name. And I was scared. I
took a step backwards and raised my hands in a conciliatory
gesture. "Whoa, man—I'm sorry," I bleated. "I don't want
no trouble with you. Lemme buy you another beer!"

Tommy stared at me for a long few seconds, and then the
tension ran out of him. He laughed, a tinkling, pleasant
laugh. "I know you, Cat," he chuckled. "You ain't as tough
as I heard, but we're going to be friends."

30

## The Cat Takes Command

We were. And with a friend like Tommy, enemies were superfluous. Tommy was a yo-yo of violent emotions. He loved to fight, and the odds were no deterrent. Once incited, Tommy was a true berserker. He fought to hurt, maim, kill —and he used whatever weapons were handy: fists, knives, knucks, clubs and what-have-you.

The slightest thing fired Tommy's volatile temper. Once when a shine boy (a man, really) didn't polish his shoes to the little gangster's satisfaction, Tommy almost beat him to death. When two other men in the shine shop interceded, Tommy gave them a brutal thrashing, too.

I was a pretty good gang brawler—I thought—but Tommy taught me dozens of new tricks.

Tommy and I pulled a lot of jobs together. Tommy was a pretty good burglar, but he preferred strong-arm robbery. Robbery by assault afforded Tommy the bodily contact, the infliction of pain, that he enjoyed. Tommy was a real weedhead. He was always hopped up—but then I was on the grass pretty good myself.

We made a pair. "The Cat and his shadow," Little Red quipped.

Age in Texas has a direct bearing on punishment of crime. Any boy under 17 cannot be sentenced to prison, no matter how serious his offense. The day he reaches 17, however, a boy is liable to all the penalties under the criminal code.

A few days after my 17th birthday, Tommy, myself and three other Black Shirts were in a roller rink. There were about 20 North Side Angels there, led by a boy called "Sandy," and the Angels began leaning on us. Tommy threw beer in Sandy's face—Tommy was fearfully wasteful of beer—and a brawl ensued. House bouncers broke up the fight and ejected the Angels.

Later that night, several gangs gathered at a drive-in restaurant for a mass rumble. Sandy and his boys were there. The Black Shirts weren't involved, but Tommy insisted we make the scene. "I want to finish it with those finks," he grated.

There were about 200 gang members from a dozen gangs at the drive-in when we arrived. The war hadn't opened because the opposing gang leaders were still arguing over rules and weapons. The manager of the drive-in was unaware of the impending rumble. He was under the happy illusion that he'd cornered the teen-age market. Tommy shattered his idyllic trance and settled the issue of weapons at the same time. He spotted Sandy and his boys near their cars. Picking up a case of empty soft drink bottles, Tommy heaved it into the ranks of the Angels and launched himself after the case of bottles.

"Here we go," I snapped to the other three Black Shirts and plunged after Tommy. The parking lot of the drive-in, and the streets around it, became a battleground. Kids spewed from their cars, shouting obscenities, and bottles began to whistle through the air, bouncing off skulls, thudding off cars and crashing through the plate glass windows of the restaurant building.

I fought my way to Tommy's side. Several Angels were sprawled around him, and he drove Sandy to the asphalt with a blow from a bottle just as I reached him. "Let's get out of here!" I screamed above the tumult. "Every cop in town will be here soon!"

We began to back out, shoulder to shoulder. Suddenly an arm encircled my neck and blows began to rain on my head. I twisted and saw an old enemy from the Podunk gang, his features contorted with angry delight. I dug my shiv from my pocket, released the blade and rammed my arm forward. I only meant to nick the boy. I felt the blade go into his body until the hilt thudded against his ribs.

The boy's eyes rolled back, his face took on a pasty pallor, and he fell away from me with a moan.

32

"Let's split," shouted Tommy, and he shoved me into the car. One other Black Shirt, a boy named Slick, leaped in with us. Tommy slammed the car in gear and dug out. We drove by a circuitous route to Hermann Park, arriving there an hour later. Tommy parked the car, sighed and reached for the bottle of wine in the glove compartment.

The spotlight hit us like a battering ram. And then two uniformed cops were in the beam, pistols leveled.

"Come out with your hands up!" one ordered.

"Ditch the shiv," Tommy said in a low voice as he swung open the door. I scrambled out, dropping the knife in the leaves. My heart was pounding. The cops snapped cuffs on us and shoved us into the back seat of the prowl car. One searched our car and the ground around it. He found the blade.

"These are the ones," he remarked grimly. "Description fits all around—boys and car. The knife has blood on it."

"What the hell are you talking about? What's the beef?" Tommy bluffed. The one cop gave him a hard look.

"Shut up, you little creep," he rapped. His next words caused a lump of ice to form in my belly.

"The kid's dead!"

# 3
# God—And a Girl

"WHO IS SHE THAT LOOKETH FORTH
AS THE MORNING, FAIR AS THE
MOON, CLEAR AS THE SUN, AND TER-
RIBLE AS AN ARMY WITH BANNERS?"
—THE SONG OF SOLOMON

The drive to the cop shop was like a ride on one of those crazy carnival coasters. My emotions ran wild with me, tilting, spinning, lurching and pitching, plunging toward the vertical edge of terror.

I had murdered a boy! And I'd die in the electric chair for my crime. My roiled reasoning could conceive of no lesser penalty.

Tommy's hand was a vise on my arm as we walked into the police station. "Play it cool," he breathed. "Don't cop to nothin'."

I wouldn't have to, I thought dully. My prints were on the knife.

There were 60 or more gang members, loose-herded by uniformed cops, in the halls outside the homicide offices. I recognized leaders of a dozen groups, and they recognized me; but nothing was said. They kept their faces carefully blank.

The patrolmen who brought us in bulled their way through the crowd, towing us behind. They confronted a grizzled, yellow-toothed detective who blocked the doorway of the homicide antiroom, placidly working a chew of tobacco. Our captors shoved us forward. "Here are your killers," one said smugly.

The detective stopped chewing his cud, and his eyebrows climbed. "Killers? Who'd they kill?"

The two cops looked perplexed. "Why we heard over our radio that some kid was knifed to death in that big gang fight. The pickup said three boys in a club coupe were suspects. These kids fill the bill all the way. We've got a bloody knife that belongs to one of them."

The detective turned his head and expelled an amber ribbon of liquidized Brown's Mule. It arched accurately into a spittoon across the room, and a pleased smile flitted across his lips. "Hell, we've taken dirks, daggers and Texas Jacks off half these little hoods, most of 'em bloody. There wasn't anyone killed in that fight. Several got sliced up, and one has a pretty good hole in his brisket; but he'll make it okay. And nobody knows nothin', naturally."

He drew his lanky form back from the doorway. "But run 'em on in. Breck wants to talk to all of 'em."

The hangman's hood was snatched from my head. The pangs of remorse vanished, too, as I walked into B. Porter's office. The gaunt lawman raked me with a flat look as I slumped into a chair. I gave him a jaunty smile. Porter nodded bleakly.

"I thought you'd be mixed up in this, kid," he said acidly. One of the policemen dropped the knife—wrapped in cellophane to preserve my fingerprints—on Porter's desk, and gave the details of our arrest.

Porter's eyes lifted from the knife to me. "Yours?" he asked.

"It's mine," said Slick. His statement was like a sudden gust of wind; it shoved us all off balance. Porter's gaze shifted to Slick, his thin face tightening. He studied Slick, who returned a mocking stare.

38

"Did you cut anyone tonight?" Porter ventured.

Slick lifted his shoulders. "I dunno. Did anyone say I did? That's my knife. You asked. I'm telling you."

A faint smile etched Porter's lips. "Tell me how old you are, while you're telling."

"I'm 15," Slick replied. His voice was maliciously bland.

Porter nodded sourly. "You would be, of course. You're also a liar, but if you want to lie yourself into the reform school that's your business."

Porter lifted a slim hand to the yellow-toothed detective. "Take him over to the juvenile detention division. I'll keep these two."

He didn't keep us long. An hour later, Tommy and I were on the street. Porter had worked us over with the lash of his tongue, welting our perverse pride, but it beat picking prison cotton. Slick rode the beef all the way. He was sent to Gatesville, convicted in juvenile court of carrying a prohibited weapon. He wasn't guilty. I was. But I let him take the rap.

I was a tenth-grade student in high school, a status attained more by subterfuge than by study. It wasn't subterfuge on my part: Some teachers weren't above doctoring my grades to get rid of me. Even so, I was booted out of several schools as an "incorrigible." Each time, my mother and my stepfather, my father and my stepmother, my grandmother or my aunt—whomever I happened to be living with at the time—would go to the school officials and plead that I be given "one more chance."

It reached the stage where "one more chance" was exactly that. There was only one high school left that would accept me. "But you're not going over there and corrupt those kids," I was warned by a school district executive. "One stunt and you've had it!"

I couldn't have corrupted anyone at that particular

39

school! It was a real jiving joint, tailored to my carnal tastes. The whole student body was hep!

The first week on campus I met Sonny.

Of all the ghosts that people my past, Sonny's haunts me most—for he was a factor in changing my life. And I was a factor in destroying his.

Sonny was an honor roll student and the dominant personality of the school. He was handsome, charming and dynamic. He was all-city football star, all-state and all-city forward on the basketball squad, a star baseball player and a three-letter man in track. There were no less than 33 colleges and universities holding out athletic scholarships to Sonny on his graduation from high school. The future, for Sonny, was a plum ripe for plucking.

But Sonny wore his mantle of fame fretfully. Whether in rebellion against his paragon's image, or in protest against some secret grievance, Sonny, beneath his shining surface, was a paradox. He flouted his athletic training rules and, instead, drank, fought and caroused. He gloried in the sensual vices and was the life of wild parties.

Sonny took a liking to me and began running around with my crowd. We offered the action he liked, in the anonymity he needed to protect his public guise. Sonny became my closest friend. I gave him the first stick of weed he ever smoked; but if I hadn't, he'd have gotten it somewhere else. Sonny was bent on paving his own road to ruin. I was only a willing helper.

"If your old man knew what you were doing, he'd blow his stack," I told Sonny.

Sonny smiled. "He won't snap," he said. He was right. Sonny's father never did snap—until it was too late.

Sonny and I started catting around with some Denver Harbor debs. He had the connections, and I had a real sharp set of wheels—a 1948 club coupe with dropped shocks, fender skirts and Hollywood pipes. It was like chromed catnip to the East End sex kittens. Sonny fixed me up with a dozen dolls, all of them geared for back seat action, but I put them down in order. I didn't know what I wanted in a girl, but whatever it was, none of them had it.

One evening, however, we walked into a hangout for high school kids, and I found what I wanted. I knew, too, that I'd reached a crossroads in my life.

A pert blonde and a petite brunette were drinking cokes at a table near the door. They both nodded at Sonny, who returned a careless wave. I saw only the dark-haired girl and the alfresco perfection of her beauty. She had a poise and loveliness that stirred a memory long erased—the memory of a brier rose unfolding to the morning. She looked at me, an impersonal look, but the casual glance was like a needle in my flesh. I grabbed Sonny's arm.

"Who's the black-haired chick?" I asked. Sonny sensed the excitement in me, but his voice was cool. "She's a sprout, Cat. Don't tamper with her. She goes to school with my sister."

Sonny's sister was 14. This girl looked 18. But 14 or 18, I had to know her. "So okay, what's her name?" I asked. Sonny shook his head. "Drop it, Cat. She's a sprout, a square sprout. Not your kind at all."

"We'll see," I said cockily, and walked over to the table. The dark-haired girl appraised me with a guarded look. The blonde raked me from my snapbrim lid to my suede shoes with sardonic eyes. "Are you The Cat?" she asked wryly.

"That's right," I said, looking at the brunette. "What's your name, doll?" The girl regarded me steadily for several seconds, then dropped her eyes. She didn't answer.

"It's none of your business," the blonde said tartly. "We know all about you, Cat. You're a weedhead, aren't you?" She began to bombard me with barbed questions until I became irritated.

"Shut up!" I rapped out. "I'm not talking to you. What

are you doing anyway, writing a book?" I turned back to her companion. She had dark eyes, full of light flecks. "Come on, what's your name?" I wheedled.

She reached down, picked up a pair of shoe skates, and rose, murmuring, "We better go," to the blonde. The fair girl flashed a sassy grin, and followed the dark-haired one out the door.

I started after them, but Sonny moved in front of me. "Drop it, Cat," he said tersely. "We're meeting some chicks, remember?"

I remembered, but I was no longer interested.

All evening, the dark-haired girl's reflection was in the mirror of my mind. I moped and brooded, thinking about her. Finally Sonny sighed and said, "Okay! Okay! Her name is Barbara. We'll go by my pad and get Sis' school directory. It's got her telephone number listed, but she's only 14 and you better not mess with her."

"I swear, I don't intend to touch her," I told Sonny. After I said it, I realized I meant it.

I called Barbara from Sonny's home. She hadn't returned from the skating rink, so we cut out for the Flick, a joint frequented by hoodlums, characters and other riff-raff. I dialed her number again as soon as we made the scene, and Barbara answered the telephone herself.

I made a frantic pitch. "This is Freddie, you know—The Cat," I blurted. "Don't hang up on me. I just want to rap with you a little, just cut up the jackpot."

"You want to *what?*" she gasped. "Talk to you, just talk," I blurted hurriedly. Then I laughed. "What's the matter, don't you understand English?"

Her voice was sharp and cool. "Not your kind. And I don't want to talk to you. You have a bad reputation, and I don't want anything to do with you."

"Look, I'm not a hood," I lied. "I know a lot of characters, and I pal around with some of them; but I'm not a weedhead, and I'm not a thug!"

"A person is known by the company he keeps," Barbara replied primly, and hung up. I was stunned. No doll had ever put me down on the phone!

I woke up the next morning and thought of Barbara first thing. She was a challenge to my ego, and I was determined to meet her again—and to know her. I knew nothing of the niceties of conventional courtship. I went about wooing Barbara with all the finesse of a lug wrench Lothario.

That afternoon I drove to Barbara's school, intending to intercept her as she left the campus. I persuaded Sonny to go with me, as I wasn't a popular figure in that particular neighborhood. We parked the car near a pool hall, across from the school, and I was recognized immediately by a dozen or more thugs. I threw up my hands, palms out, as they moved toward us.

"Cool it," I yelped. "I ain't here to beef. I came to see a hide."

"Yeah, The Cat's all hung up over that little Barbara," Sonny added with a placating smile. Several of the toughs followed us as we cut over to the school.

I spotted Barbara emerging from the school building, but she wasn't alone. A tall, good-looking boy walked beside her, carrying her books. I watched, surprised, as he handed her into a car with casual gallantry. A derisive voice behind me piped, "If that's your hide, Cat, some square John is cutting you out."

I hurried over to the car and Barbara looked up, amazement clouding her eyes. Her escort, in the act of starting the car, looked up. "What's the score?" he asked, looking at Barbara.

I gestured with my hand. "I ain't here for trouble," I told him, looking at Barbara. "I came to take you home."

Her dark eyes sparked. "That's news to me," she gritted. "I wouldn't be caught dead with you! Let's go, Glen." Glen's hand moved to the gear shift.

I exploded. I drew my shiv and grabbed Glen's shoulder. "You stay away from her," I hissed. "She's my girl!"

Barbara's hands flew to her mouth and Glen paled. Then he knocked my hand away, rolled up the car window, and dug out—with Barbara glaring angrily back at me. Sonny chuckled wickedly. "Well, that did it," he drawled. "You can sure forget her, now."

I glared at him, angry and baffled, and walked back to my own car. That evening I called Barbara to apologize. She wouldn't speak to me. Her mother got on the phone and warned me to stay away from Barbara and not to bother her again.

I didn't heed the warning. Instead, I embarked on a ruthless campaign to force Barbara's capitulation. I got a hood to beat up Glen. Several guys who were dating Barbara took the hint and quit seeing her.

I took some boys myself and crashed a party she attended later that week. We had a big beef with the square Johns and broke up the party. Barbara was furious. I grabbed her, and she broke into angry tears and struggled to get away; but I held her and told her, "I don't like this any better than you do, but I'm a persistent guy, and I'm going to keep it up until you see me and talk to me!"

Barbara jerked free. "I don't want anything to do with you," she blazed. "You've already got the whole school talking about me!"

I sought out Sonny for advice. "I've known some square chicks, but this Barbara is something else again," I said, disconsolate. "She's so square, it's like she'd been born in a box."

"Why don't you quit pushing her so hard?" Sonny

44

offered. "She's not one of your way-out Mollies. She never will be."

I'd already decided I couldn't coerce Barbara's affection, so I took Sonny's advice and dropped the rough stuff. But every afternoon, I was at Barbara's school to confront her and make a pitch. For two weeks, she ignored all my pleas, and then one afternoon she came out and said, "Take me home."

I was elated, but once in the car, she quickly put a damper on my hopes. "Freddie, you've got to stop this, please," she implored. "If you really care for me, you won't embarrass me again. We're not the same type of people, you and I."

I put down a frantic hype. I confessed I'd been wrong, but I begged her to forgive my past mistakes. I promised her I'd do nothing to offend her if she'd only see me. "Just give me a chance," I pleaded. Barbara shook her head. "I'm afraid it wouldn't work, Freddie," she sighed. I sensed she was wavering, however, and continued to argue my case.

There was a boy sitting in a car, waiting for her, when we reached her home. "It looks like I'm going to have a big crew to assassinate," I remarked ruefully. Barbara laughed. "Good-bye, Freddie. Please don't try to see me again."

I didn't answer. I knew I'd try to see Barbara again. I had to: I was in love with her. The knowledge left me both delighted and dejected, for I knew Barbara wasn't in love with me. I was, however, on a much better footing with her, and that was a consolation.

My state of happy torment endured for three weeks, and then I hit upon a clever scheme. Blind dates were the fad among the high school set. I persuaded one of Barbara's girlfriends to get Barbara a blind date with me. We arranged to meet after school, since I didn't want to risk a scene at her home.

45

Barbara flipped when she saw me and learned that I was her date; but then the humor of the ruse dispelled her irritation and she consented to the date. We went to a drive-in movie.

It was the beginning of a tumultuous relationship. We had several dates without incident, and I was careful to conform to Barbara's standards of conduct. I was still continuing my illicit activities, however, with no intention of reforming; and I became overconfident as Barbara's regard for me grew. I introduced her to Tommy and some of my other hoodlum associates, and took her to several character hangouts. Barbara was dubious about these excursions into an alien world; and when Tommy and I got into a beef with some squares one night, she bucked.

"I'm through, Freddie," Barbara said bitterly. "This isn't my kind of life, and these aren't my kind of people. You're a hoodlum. Find yourself another girl, because you won't change."

She meant it, I learned after calling her several times during the following week. I was miserable at first, then angry, when I learned that she was dating other boys. Galveston, on the Gulf of Mexico below Houston, annually opens its tourist season with a "Splash Day" celebration. I had planned to take Barbara to the "Splash Day" pageant of 1950, but she went with another boy. I was put down.

"I know the square John she's with," Tommy growled. "Let's go find them. I'll fix that creep!"

My jealous anger overrode what good judgment I possessed. Tommy and I drove to Galveston to search out Barbara and her date. We spotted the boy's sleek convertible on West Beach. The boy was asleep in the front seat. Barbara was frolicking in the ocean.

Tommy's actions were typical. He gave the boy a savage beating. Then he slashed the top of the convertible, the seats

46

and the tires of the car to ribbons with his knife. Tommy was regarding his brutal handiwork when Barbara returned to the car. She stopped, stunned, and then the shock in her dark eyes was replaced by angry contempt. "Get out of here!" she cried. "I never want to see you again. Ever!"

"That suits me," I barked, and Tommy and I cut out. Driving back to Houston, however, remorse seized me; and I burned with shame at our actions. I suddenly saw myself as Barbara saw me, and I wasn't pleased with the portrait.

I cast about for ways to bridge the chasm between us, but Barbara was adamant. She wouldn't see me, and she wouldn't talk to me on the telephone. I was ready to accept any terms she laid down.

Barbara was an avid skater and went regularly to a certain rink. I was there every night she skated, but she resolutely ignored my presence. It was at the rink that I became fully aware of how I had affected her life. Barbara, in dating me, had stamped herself as a hep doll. When she put me down, there were other eyes that saw her dark beauty and they weren't sentimental eyes.

I became chillingly aware of this one night as I sat at a table with Tommy, drinking beer and morosely eyeing Barbara as she flashed about the rink.

Tony, a hood I knew, and three well-dressed men took a table next to us. I recognized the three as big-time procurers, men who supplied call girls to high circles in a dozen Texas cities and who had vested interests in several bawdy houses that catered to the common trade. I nodded to Tony, wondered briefly why he was with the three and then dismissed them from my mind. Then, perhaps an hour later, Barbara paused at the rink railing near us. One of the men with Tony whistled softly. "I've been watching that girl," he drawled. "I'm going to turn her out. I'll make a million dollars off her!"

I was on my feet and at his side without thinking. I cursed him wickedly. "If you so much as speak to her, I'll kill you!"

I knew how he turned out girls like Barbara: a drug in their coke to knock them out, a motel room to hold them prisoner and a straightened-out coat hanger to whip them into submission while he taught them the arts of the world's oldest profession!

The white slaver—he was just a pimp to me—looked up at me, his eyes cold and glittering. His right hand dipped inside his coat. I knew I was up tight, but I didn't care. I tensed, ready to cut his throat if he came out with a gun. A red mist blanketed my brain.

"Wait a minute!" Tony's voice sliced through the tension, sharp as an Arctic wind. "Is that your girl, Cat?"

I nodded, never taking my eyes off the man I intended to kill.

"Then lay off her," the big outlaw rasped to his companion. "All of you, understand?"

The pimp glared venomously at me, and then his hand emerged slowly from his coat, empty. "I was just kiddin'," he muttered surlily. I threw Tony a grateful look and turned away, a tremble in my legs.

Later, as Tommy and I were leaving, Tony stopped me.

"Why don't you snap, kid?" he said in low tones. "You don't belong in the rackets. You never have. Take my advice, kid, and square up. Marry your girl and live a decent life—it'd be the best thing that ever happened to you!"

I nodded and thanked him. I knew one thing for certain: If I stuck around, I sure wasn't going to deal in girls. I discarded that ambition that night!

Several weeks later, I met Barbara at a skating rink in Galveston. I pleaded with her to allow me to drive her home to Houston, and she reluctantly agreed.

I poured out my woes on the drive back, and I excoriated

myself. I admitted I'd been a hoodlum most of my life, and was one now. "But I swear I'll pull up!" I said desperately. "You can square me up. But without you—I don't stand a chance."

Barbara studied me, tears welling in her eyes. Then she put her head on my shoulder and cried. "I hope you will, Freddie," she said in a muffled voice, "because I love you!" I drove a mile before I realized what she had said, and then the gates of my joy flew wide!

I really did try to square up, but it takes more than the love of a good woman—and Barbara was still a child, really—to change a man. He has to want to change, and I soon admitted I didn't want to change. The wild, exciting, frantic life still appealed to me. I began leading a dual existence. I'd take Barbara out, spend a sedate evening with her and then take her home at midnight. Then I'd meet Tommy, Sonny or others and party until daybreak. Barbara learned of my relapse, of course, and raised heated objections; but I beat her down with more promises to "square up."

Then the seed Tony planted sprouted. I began talking marriage to Barbara. She was dubious at first, and her parents flatly opposed any such marriage; but I won Barbara over, and a sympathetic aunt persuaded her parents to give their permission.

We were married September 1, 1950. I was 17 and Barbara was 15. Even the preacher who administered the vows had his doubts that the marriage would endure. "It'll never work out, never!" one relative predicted ominously.

I threw a party in a nightclub following the wedding reception. Every hood in town who wasn't in jail made the scene. Whiskey, wine and beer, as well as champagne, went down by the hogshead, and those who didn't get high on the lush got loaded on hemp and heroin. The vice squad could have picked in tall cotton that night.

Barbara didn't join in the revelry to any extent. "Don't worry, Honey," I assured her. "This is the last time we'll see these people! From now on, I'm a square John!"

I moved Barbara into an apartment, got a job and settled down to a square life.

"I can make it," I boasted on the first day.

On the second day, I wasn't so sure.

On the third day, a bunch of characters dropped by the apartment after I came home from work, and the corners were knocked off my square. We had a blast, although Barbara was scared. She was fearful that I'd return to the wild bunch, and she was right. I quit my job and got another. I quit that job after a few days and went back to hustling and stealing. Our apartment became a hood hangout over Barbara's vehement protests, and our domestic bliss began evaporating.

Barbara was mature beyond her years. Marriage, to her, meant having a home, an honest job, children, a savings account and a plan for the future—all the little things that, taken together, form the coronet of happiness for a woman.

Marriage, to me, meant having Barbara all to myself—a strictly selfish view. I hadn't the vaguest idea of the responsibilities of marriage, or the sacred sanctions involved. Confronted with them, I lacked the moral courage and strength to measure up to my vows.

I treated Barbara cruelly and shamefully. I lied to her and slapped and beat her on several occasions. I tried to change her to my way of life; and when I failed, I began staying out late at night, drinking, using dope and consorting with other women. I wallowed in corruption.

Barbara fought to save her marriage—and me—with every weapon she possessed. Three times she left me, and three times she returned—hopeful of salvaging the life she sought for us. The fourth month of our marriage, I shed the last vestiges of pride. We argued, and I beat her. Not with my fists. I used the pimp method: I took a belt and whipped her unmercifully. It didn't break her spirit, but it smashed any hopes she had of saving our marriage. She packed her bags.

"I'm through with you and your hoodlums," she said with cold finality. I looked into her pain-filled eyes and knew that she meant what she was saying. I had destroyed the most beautiful thing in my life. My shame and remorse ate like acid at my conscience, but all I said was, "So get out!" She did.

I suffocated my remorse in the smoke of the weed, and I buried my conscience in the muck of my misdoing. I was a hitchhiker on the highway to hell.

One afternoon Dad came to my apartment. I was surprised, not only at the visit but at the change in him. He was not the roistering father I'd known all my life. He was a different man, soft-spoken and quietly confident—a man at peace with himself and the world.

Dad explained the transformation. God had wrought it, Dad said simply—through His servant, the Reverend Dan Vestal, a Baptist evangelist.

"I have accepted Christ," Dad told me. "I've quit drinking and carrying on. I know I haven't been a good father to you, but I'm concerned about you now. I want you to go to services with me."

I scoffed at him. Me, in church? Why, every character in Houston would put me down if they heard I was attending church! Sure, I believed there was a God, I knew there was a God, but I didn't know Him and He didn't know me, and I sure wasn't inclined to get acquainted at this late stage. "Thanks, but no thanks," I told Dad bitterly.

Dad left, but he came back. In fact, he bugged me for weeks to attend the revival. Brother Vestal, said Dad, was nearing the end of his visit to Houston, and Dad felt certain my life would be changed if I'd only go hear Vestal preach. I declined each time.

Reverend Vestal's last services were held on a Sunday

night. It was sleeting and raining that day, and several characters and their girls had taken refuge in my apartment. We were lazing around, belting beer, when Dad came calling again. There was a determined cast to his jaws. "Now look, Dad, I've told you I'm not going to hear that preacher pound my ear, so lay off, will ya?" I protested.

Dad smiled, an odd smile. "You're going tonight, son. You're going to go, or you're going to fight me all over Houston!" Dad meant it, I realized. He sounded like B. Porter.

"Okay, I'll go, but just this once, hear?" I said sulkily.

"Just this once," Dad agreed, and I thought he was going to hug me. "We'll pick you up here."

I shooed the hoods and broads out, telling them I'd meet them later, at a certain club, and then got all sharped up for my church debut. I dressed in my best threads—sharkskin suit, alligator shoes, snapbrim beaver lid and camel's hair topcoat. I felt like I'd looted a menagerie, but I figured I'd knock out the eyes of the hypocrites and phonies at the church.

Dad and my stepmother called for me at 7. I was surprised when I slid into the backseat of the car—Barbara was with them! My stepmother had persuaded her to come, I learned later.

"You going to sing in the choir?" I said sarcastically.

"I'm going to sing," she replied quietly.

"You got your prayer book, baby?" I kept the needle in her. She looked at me impassively and lifted her hand. She was holding a Bible.

Reverend Vestal's revival was at the Melrose Baptist Church on Humble Road. Services were about to begin when we arrived, but I stood outside and smoked a cigarette before going in. Dad, Barbara and my stepmother were sitting down front, and I thought sourly that Dad had gotten ringside seats for the occasion. I took a seat in the back row.

After a while, Dad looked around, saw me, and then brought Barbara and my stepmother to the back of the church to sit with me. Dad started introducing me to people around us.

The congregation started singing. I didn't join in. I maintained a skeptical mien, but I knew in my heart there had to be something to it. Then a young girl stood up and sang a solo—"It's No Secret What God Can Do"—in a sweet, tinkling voice; and something stirred inside me, like the vague pains of hunger. I shifted in my seat and fought the feeling.

Then Reverend Vestal stepped to the pulpit. I was shocked. He wasn't really a big man, but he loomed huge behind the pulpit. He wore a tailored sharkskin suit, with a loud tie streaming down the front of his shirt and a gaudy handkerchief ballooning out of the breast pocket of his coat. A large scar marred the left side of his face, and he had combed his hair in a way that attempted to hide part of the mark. He made a ludicrous figure, I thought sulkily.

Then he looked right at me and began to speak, and my scalp tingled. The man had a voice like a silver trumpet! "You must be born again!" he said, holding me with his eyes. "I do not mean you should make a new start or turn over a new leaf. I mean you must be born again, with a new heart!"

Dan Vestal paused, but his compassionate eyes did not waver from mine. I wanted to look away, but I couldn't. "We are all born wrong," he went on. "But we can be born a second time. That which is born of the flesh is flesh, but that which is born of the Spirit is spirit. God has told us this—and I tell you this!"

The big man did not take his eyes from me, it seemed, as he told of people who had tried to reform and failed because they had not made Christ a part of their reformation. His clarion voice filled the church, washing over me, and every time he pointed to emphasize something, he seemed to point right at me! I stole a glance at Dad and Barbara, and thought angrily that they'd bum-rapped me to this big preacher. They'd finked on me, and he had built his sermon around me.

"There are only 12 inches between heaven and hell," Vestal said in his booming, melodious voice; and his ham-size hand tapped his heart and his head. "The difference between heart belief and head belief!"

I struggled against the spell he was weaving, but I was drowning in his voice.

Then that man, marked with his terrible scar, took me to the Cross. He took me to Jerusalem, and I saw Jesus reviled and spat upon, delivered to the Romans, scourged and given a crown of thorns, and crucified! The picture Vestal painted was so vivid—I felt he had been there.

Vestal's voice continued to mesmerize me: "Salvation is not something you do—but something God does! Going to church doesn't make you a Christian any more than going to a stable makes you a horse. Too many of you are professors, not possessors. But I say to you who stand behind hypocrites and call them small, that you are smaller. Else you couldn't stand behind them!"

I was being stripped of my armor of cynicism. As he talked, I thought of my past life and was suddenly appalled. My sins and misdeeds marched in review as Vestal talked, and Caesar's legions were less numerous. I was immersed in shame and misery when Vestal finished his sermon and asked the congregation to bow their heads in prayer. I dropped my head in shame, for I did not know how to pray. My father, I thought dully, had destroyed me by forcing me to come here.

"Will those who are saved lift their hands?" Vestal asked with a slight smile. I was watching him from beneath my lowered lids, and I glanced surreptitiously at Barbara. She hadn't lifted her hand either, I noticed; and I was surprised.

But she was crying. "Will those who have not accepted Christ lift their hands?" Vestal asked. I lifted mine. So did Barbara. Then the choir started singing softly, "Just As I Am," and Vestal spoke again: "Will you accept Christ? He will accept you, just as you are." Vestal continued to entreat those who had not been saved to come forward, and my Dad, my stepmother and several others urged me to walk down to the altar. I wanted to, but I couldn't.

A boy whispered to Vestal, and the big man listened intently. Then he straightened up and announced, "There is a boy here we've been praying for. If he comes to Christ, hundreds of young people will come to God." The big preacher left the pulpit and lumbered down the aisle, searching right and left. I cringed as he stopped at my row, studied me a moment and then leaned over and placed his thick arm around me. It lay on my shoulder like a feather.

"Would you like to become a Christian, son?" he asked. There was no pressure in his voice.

I shook my head. "I can't live up to it!"

Vestal smiled. "No," he said gently. "You can't live up to it! If you could live up to it, there would be no need of your being saved, would there?"

He closed his eyes, and I knew he was praying. I clenched my hands over the back of the pew in front of me and wished I knew how to pray, too. And then a tear came from beneath Vestal's right eyelid, rolled down across that terrible scar and splashed on the back of my hand. It scalded my skin like boiling water, and suddenly I wanted this man's Jesus.

I was down front, and Barbara was with me, and Reverend Vestal was intoning Romans 10:9 in an exultant voice: "That if thou shalt confess with thy mouth the Lord Jesus, and shalt believe in thine heart that God hath raised Him from the dead, thou shalt be saved."

I didn't know how to confess, but I prayed the best I

knew how, and as I stumbled through my mumbled plea, begging forgiveness, I felt the breath of God on my cheek.

I rose clean and refreshed, and Barbara was beside me. She was looking at me with radiant eyes that brimmed with tears of happiness. I looked at her and found her more beautiful than ever.

"We're going to live for God," I said; and for the first time, I believed my own words. So did Barbara.

Dad and my stepmother were weeping for joy, and people were hugging me and pumping my hands. I broke free and sought out Vestal. He was smiling, and I knew suddenly that he was not even aware of that scar, which now was of no consequence.

"What did that boy whisper to you?" I asked.

Reverend Vestal's lips twisted in a gentle smile. "He said, 'The Cat is in the back.' Is that what they call you?"

I nodded and laughed, sharing his amusement. We would laugh together again over the incident. After all, thousands of preachers had found "lost sheep"; but how many had brought a cat into the fold?

# 4

## "Moses in the Lion's Den!"

"THE GREAT END OF LIFE IS
NOT KNOWLEDGE BUT ACTION."
—THOMAS HUXLEY

I hadn't been saved 72 hours when I set out to resurrect the church. I had felt its pulse and pronounced it dead. It wasn't an accurate diagnosis, but at the time my zeal to serve the Lord far exceeded my knowledge and judgment. I am sure there were both winces and smiles in Heaven over my antics those first few days.

Jesus had fired the furnace of my soul, and when I walked from Melrose Baptist Church the night I made my decision for Christ, I felt called to preach the Gospel of Jesus Christ.

The moment Barbara and I reached home, I grabbed the telephone and started calling people. I called my grandmother. I called a man who had shown me kindness in years past. I called several teachers and principals who had sought to help me during my guerrilla war with education.

"I've been saved!" I told each one of them. Each was happy to get the surprising news, and all wished me well. All, that is, except my grandmother. She had never believed I was in any danger that warranted saving. But she was glad I'd gone to church.

I received a telephone call, too. Rocky, one of the characters that I'd promised to meet later that night called from the nightclub where we'd arranged a rendezvous. "What's holding you up, man? We're having a blast!" he shouted.

"I'm not coming," I told him. "I've found a better way to live, man!"

"What've you been smoking, Cat?" Rocky asked suspiciously. "You ain't had a fix, have you?"

"Yeah, I have," I exulted. "I've had a shot of Jesus! I've been born again, Rocky, and it's great!" I tried to tell him of the wondrous thing that had happened to me, but he interrupted with a knowing laugh.

"Okay, okay!" he chided me. "So you're on a religious kick. You'll shake it in three weeks—then you'll be around again." The receiver clicked in my ear.

I was touched by despair as I turned to Barbara.

"How can I tell them?" I cried out. "How am I going to get them saved?"

Barbara ran to me and threw her arms about me. "You'll know," she whispered against my shoulder. "The Lord will let you know!"

And suddenly I did know. Rocky was right. I would be around again. I wouldn't leave the underworld. I'd set up a pulpit in its shadows!

There would be a delay, I realized with regret in almost the same instant, for there was something I first had to do—something my heart urged and my mind resisted. I did it, however. The next morning I drove to the police station and, with a hammerlock on the hoodlum in me, sought out a lieutenant of detectives. He knew me. He had handled me several times for juvenile offenses, and he'd always treated me fairly. He was fair now. He listened attentively as I told of my salvation and my desire to go and preach the Gospel of Christ. Then I took the icy plunge.

"I came here to tell you about the jobs I've pulled," I blurted. "Some of them I can pinpoint, and some I can't. There were others with me on all but one or two of the capers."

60

I paused and eyed him stubbornly. "I ain't going to fink on the others. Not even the Lord wants me to be a stool pigeon. I feel that. But I'll cop to my part in all of them, and I'm ready to go to the joint. Maybe it won't be for long," I added miserably. I hoped he'd let me call Barbara after we'd finished, and I wondered how I was going to break the bad news.

The lieutenant's features were set in a thoughtful mien, and I saw myself being weighed in the scales of his eyes. He pulled a stubby pipe from his pocket and began to pack it while skepticism and belief warred within him.

"You put me in a tough spot, son," he murmured. "The law is a funny thing. It says a guilty person should be punished for his crime. You're about to confess to some crimes, so according to the law, you'll have to be punished."

The lieutenant put a match to his bowl of tobacco and continued, expelling his words in a cloud of smoke. "But the law also says that where more than one are involved in a crime, all are equally guilty and, by the law, subject to equal punishment. Now, you're not going to tell me the names of the others involved in these crimes, so they can't be punished as you will be. Doesn't seem fair to you or the law, does it?"

I didn't answer. I don't think he expected me to answer. He puffed away at his pipe and spoke again. "To get back to the law, it says that the purpose of punishment—sending a man to prison, that is—is rehabilitation. To reform him. If what you have told me is true, and I believe it is, you have already been reformed." The lieutenant's lips pursed musingly. "In fact, you've been reborn—you're another person, and to try you for the crimes Freddie, The Cat committed would just be wasting the time of some busy judges and juries, to my way of looking at the law."

The lieutenant cut little flourishes in the air with the stem of his pipe, like a fencer flexing his blade.

"I'm not sure you could tell me of any jobs we don't

already suspect you of," he commented wryly. "And what you'd prove for us with a confession wouldn't get you more than five years, in all probability, when a jury sees your baby mug."

The lieutenant nodded—his decision was made. "Don't tell me anything, kid. Get out of here, and let this be between me and you and the Man upstairs. If you're on His team, you'll do more good for the law than sittin' in a cell for five years."

I stared at him numbly. I couldn't believe the man would stick his neck out for me like this; and then I did believe it, and I felt like both laughing and crying. I did not have the words to adequately thank him; but I mumbled something, squeezed his hand and started to leave.

"One thing, son," the lieutenant added as I reached the door. His still look was like a bright javelin poised between us. "I'm probably wrong about all that law I spouted. I'm a cop, not a lawyer—don't let me be wrong about you!"

I met his look firmly. "You won't be, Lieutenant, I promise!" I vowed and, closing the door behind me, I fled down the stairs and outside. I felt good as I walked to my car—and I felt clean. I was clean. I had a freshly-laundered soul and a washed-and-ironed conscience!

The grapevine—with that mysterious swiftness that surpasses Western Union in relaying information—had spread the word of my conversion throughout the North Side. I stopped at the cleaners to pick up a suit, and the owner greeted me with a smile and pumped my hand.

"You've always had a lot of influence on the kids on this side of town," he said. "It wasn't the right kind of influence. But you've got a new kind of power to use now, and I hope you do something with it."

"Man, I'll do anything to help save these kids who are taking the same road I traveled," I replied vehemently—and I meant it.

## "Moses in the Lion's Den!"

My fervor to serve God had not diminished. I testified for Christ even before I was baptized—at services that night at a Baptist church. Barbara and I were baptized the following Wednesday night, an event some members of the congregation remember vividly because a horde of hoodlums descended on the church to witness my baptism.

They sprawled in the church pews, grinning derisively, as Barbara and I were purified in the ancient ceremony of immersion. Several of them waited outside and gathered around when Barbara and I left the church.

"Hey, Cat, lemme feel your wings!" one gibed. The others made similar barbed remarks. All of them were convinced I wouldn't stay "squared up."

Many church people were of the same opinion. My past was a mountain that wouldn't soon be reduced to a molehill in their eyes. They accepted me with an aloof reserve. I realized that I was a misfit in their midst.

I also disrupted the staid harmony of many parishioners' religious lives. The pastor of another church asked me to testify at a youth rally being held at his church, and I agreed. Some of the kids who belonged to the church decided to promote my appearance. They tacked up posters all over the neighborhood and persuaded the editor of the now-defunct *North Side Citizen* to print a story about me. The church couldn't seat all the people who showed up that Sunday night.

I told them what they'd come to hear—the details of my lurid past. I didn't mitigate my misdeeds, but I shocked them when I charged them with being partly responsible for my crimes and the activities of other kids like me.

"You sit here, Sunday after Sunday, secure and warm in your church and your Christianity," I shouted. "You don't know what's going on outside—and you're not really interested in knowing!

"Where were you church people, you church kids, when I

63

needed you? Why didn't you seek me out and witness to me? I never knew you existed until my Dad dragged me into a church.

"The kids that belong to the street gangs aren't going to come to church—most of them don't even know what a church is. You've got to go out and find them. Or are you afraid to witness on the street corners, in the beer joints and dives, and in the alleys and gutters?

"God didn't save you to sit down and sit—he saved you to get up and get! So let's get with it!"

Scores came to the altar following my testimony, and 27 young people and adults accepted Christ that night. As a result of that service, too, the Youth Crusade of the North Side Baptist churches was born. It is still continuing.

As I drove home that night, I felt that I had made my first restitution to Christ.

The next several months were critical months for me, months during which my resolve, determination and fortitude were tested again and again.

I led a rigorous life, for I worked during the day as a truck driver for the *Houston Press,* a newspaper which in the past had bannered accounts of several of my crimes; and at night I appeared in various Houston-area churches, testifying for God.

My actions and my activities were watched closely by both the lawful and the lawless; and I often realized, looking out into a sea of faces, that I was still on probation. At times, while speaking, I would be struck by the number of faces that reflected disbelief, suspicion, distrust or open hostility.

I was surprised at the number of police officers who attended church. They were regular members of the congregations to which they belonged, although one or two admitted that they had come especially to hear me and to weigh my sincerity. None of them, however, made any attempts to harass me, and none offered any overt criticism. Most of them, in fact, encouraged me and were ready to help me in any way they could. If any of them thought I was "playing an angle," they kept such an opinion secret.

There was an "angle" being worked, but not by me. I was still a sharp dresser. I still wore a "ducktail" haircut, popular with the wild teen set at the time, and I still used the underworld jargon in talking.

My hep appearance and my jive talk fascinated a lot of people, and many preachers who invited me to speak from their pulpits played up the hoodlum angle to get the crowds.

There were other pastors—and lay workers, too—who, while they liked these results, didn't like the methods. My "Cat" talk offended them, and my enthusiasm worried them. They tried to temper my tongue and moderate my eagerness, but succeeded only in angering me. I felt I was being knocked more by the Pharisees than by the Publicans.

"Listen," I snapped. "If you church people had spent as much time trying to save me as you are trying to cool me off, I wouldn't be a problem to you now!"

In my ardor, I felt the church as a whole was too formal and too complacent—and that too many of its members were concerned more with social niceties and conventions than with saving souls and serving the Lord.

"The Gospel isn't something you come to church to hear," I charged. "The Gospel is something you go from church to tell!"

I believed that then, and I believe that now. Barbara and I had joined the Victory Baptist Church, and within six weeks I was made the training union director. Attendance in the training union suddenly became higher than in Sunday school. Then I was elected president of the Young Peoples' Department. The membership tripled within a few weeks.

But I wanted to preach—to spread the Gospel. The compulsion was so strong that I began badgering the pastor to assist me in becoming ordained. He was at first reluctant —not so much because of my background, as because of my age—but one day I declared: "Pastor, I'm going to preach. I'll preach on the street corners if I can't preach in the churches—but I'm going to preach for Jesus!"

The pastor discussed my request with the board of deacons and then presented my plea to the membership for a vote. Five months after I received Christ, I was licensed to preach His glory!

Rarely has a soldier of the Lord set forth to battle so ill-equipped. My knowledge of the Bible was skimpy and not too clearly understood. My theological "education" consisted of a book I'd read on the life of Billy Sunday (a book which had crystallized my desire to preach), and I was not articulate at all in the King's "square" English. But I was armored in the righteousness of my cause, armed with the sword of His truth, and I ventured out unafraid.

My sermons were not carefully thought out and rehearsed. I shot from the hip and documented my preachments on evil from my own experiences. I did use illustrations from the Scriptures, but a lot of the words in the Bible were tongue-tanglers to me. I didn't let it bother me: When I'd encounter a difficult word, I'd turn to the regular pastor and frankly ask, "How do you pronounce that word, man?"

I cracked up some congregations. One night, after a particularly fiery sermon (or so I thought) which I had based on my Bible study, I turned from the pulpit to find the pastor struggling to control his laughter. In fact, the entire congregation was fighting the giggles.

"What's the matter?" I asked, puzzled. "Didn't you like my sermon?"

"It was a fine sermon, son—fine," he said, patting my shoulder. "But it was not Moses who was thrown into the lion's den, it was Daniel!"

There were other congregations that did not find me

amusing at all because I flayed them for their tendency to let well enough alone and lashed them for their contentment.

"This isn't a church," I thundered at several startled flocks. "It's a 'bless-me' club, a social club, a country club!

"You sing 'Standing on the Promises' of the Lord, but you're doing nothing but sitting on His premises. A chicken, when she sits, at least hatches out something. You people have been sitting for 25 years and haven't hatched anything yet!

"You've got to shine like a diamond on a coal pile, people! Jesus said, 'Ye shall be witnesses'—so get out and witness!"

In one church where I preached on several occasions, the organist—during my sermons—wrote down all my grammatical errors as I talked. Then she approached me holding her list.

"You said, 'I have saw' when you should have said, 'I have seen,' " she began. I stopped her at that point.

"I'd rather hear somebody say, 'I have saw' that had seen something, than to hear them say, 'I have seen' when they hadn't seen anything," I replied. "You're worried about cleaning up my grammar when you've got cobwebs in the baptistry." It wasn't a figure of speech. There *were* cobwebs in the baptistry.

At another church, a lady stood up in the midst of the congregation and challenged me. "A good shepherd feeds his sheep," she stated. "When are you going to start feeding us? All you've done so far is skin us!"

I told her why. "You can't feed a dead sheep—you have to skin it!" I declared.

The newspapers began taking notice of the furor I was engendering. One story began: "Freddie Gage, a budding young evangelist who renounced his criminal associates for Christ, either makes his listeners glad, sad or mad. . . ."

I had no quarrel with the story as a whole, but I had not renounced my criminal associates—only my life of crime and corruption. As I had vowed the night I was redeemed, I was quite active in the underworld—on behalf of God. Since few of my former companions appeared at the services I conducted in the various churches, I sought them out in the haunts which they frequented and which I knew so well myself. I'd walk into a beer tavern, pool hall or nightclub, spot some of the characters I used to run with, pull up a chair, open my Bible and start talking. The first few times I invaded character hangouts, I was met with snickers, ridicule and sarcasm; but as I persisted the disdain vanished, and they'd sit quietly as I preached the glory of Christ and urged them to accept Him.

"You shouldn't come into places like this, Cat," one rebuked me. Then a wistful tone crept into his voice. "I wish you had a church of your own. I don't dig religion, but I'd come."

"I do have a church—it's right here!" I shot back. "And you can make a decision for Christ right here."

He didn't, but there were hundreds who did. Paul Carlin was one. Paul not only accepted Christ, but became a servant of the Lord; and today he is one of the South's most dedicated young evangelists. Unfortunately, most of those whom I sought to salvage did not abide by their decisions. They returned, after a short period, to their criminal pursuits and the pleasures and foibles of the flesh that had ruled them all their lives. I was disappointed time and again, as much in the church clergy and laity as in the recidivists— for many of these dope fiends, prostitutes, drunkards and hoodlums would not have regressed had there been available adequate follow-up contacts, with spiritual counseling and a strong hand to steady them.

Men's souls, like different types of metal, must be hardened and tempered under different temperatures and conditions in God's forge—where the tungsten is not faith, but charity.

## "Moses in the Lion's Den!"

It seemed to me that too many churchmen, clergy and lay alike, were opposed to my preaching in pool halls, witnessing in taverns and mingling with my former companions in crime. They were regarded by most Christians as social outcasts.

"I was a social outcast, too," I argued. "And Jesus Christ spent most of his ministry on earth among social outcasts. He was one himself!"

I felt that my activities had the full sanction of God. I spent many hours praying for the guidance and strength I needed in my mission, and I always arose with my desires refreshed and my convictions confirmed. Reverend Dan Vestal supported my efforts to take the Cross into the wilderness of the underworld—and, gradually, so did other clergymen, businessmen and civic leaders who came to recognize the need for church-supported institutions or movements to combat narcotics addiction, juvenile delinquency and all other forms of criminality.

Reverend Vestal had maintained a close contact with me from the night he led me to Christ. I learned that the day following my conversion, driving home to Forth Worth, Reverend Vestal and another preacher accompanying him had prayed for me over every mile of the journey. Thereafter, Reverend Vestal often wrote me encouraging letters, called me long distance or sought me out, when he was in Houston, to hearten me and counsel me. His personal interest in me (which Reverend Vestal accredits to Christ) has had a definite and constructive influence on the course of my life since.

In the first glow of my ministry, I resisted suggestions that I further my education by attending a theological seminary. I didn't feel I needed any theological training to preach to characters. Reverend Vestal, Barbara, the pastor of my church and his wife, and a handful of others convinced me that I was being dogmatic.

69

"Christ did preach to social outcasts, as you say," it was pointed out to me, "but he did not limit his ministry to social outcasts. And he didn't call you to preach to a limited group, either. To be a real clergyman, to reach the masses, you must have a real knowledge of the Bible and a command of the language that will enable you to communicate with all the people. You can't go on bum-rapping Moses by throwing him into the lion's den!"

I was persuaded to enroll in Decatur Baptist College, located in Decatur, near Forth Worth. Barbara was delighted. She had never admonished me, but I knew that I had embarrassed her on several occasions with my drastic performances.

Barbara and I drove to Decatur several days before the beginning of the spring semester. I did some praying on that drive, and Barbara confessed later that she did, too. I was nervous and doubtful, for I didn't know how I would be received, and my apprehension increased when we arrived and we found the local newspaper had heralded my coming. HOUSTON YOUTH WHO DIGS JIVE ENROLLS IN BAPTIST COLLEGE proclaimed the headline of the front-page story. The story detailed my shady past, my activities in Houston and my ambitions—and was altogether accurate. But I hoped it hadn't riled any of the college officials. I had assumed that they would prefer to keep my presence on the campus quiet, and the less said about me, the better.

I had assumed wrong.

I did feel out of place and uncomfortable during my first few days, but it was not the fault of the student body or faculty. The registrar treated me no differently than any other new student, the other freshmen greeted me cordially and without undue curiosity, and the president of the college, Otis Strickland, made an effort to put me at ease and let me know in various ways that to him I was just another ministerial student.

"Moses in the Lion's Den!"

"These square Christians are all right!" I exclaimed to Barbara, who merely smiled.

I wanted to take all Bible courses, but Reverend Vestal and others prevailed on me to take a balanced curriculum, including English.

I found it difficult to establish strict study habits and soon was regretting my poor record in high school and the years I had wasted improving my criminal techniques when I could have been improving my mind.

One evening, less than a month after I had enrolled, I was sweating over my textbooks when there was a knock on the door. I opened it to find two young men standing there. One smiled and introduced himself and his friend.

"We've heard about you, Brother Gage," he said, "and we were wondering if you could come speak at our church."

"You bet," I replied. "God called me to preach!"

My acceptance established a pattern. By day I was a ministerial student. At night and on weekends I preached in various churches in Decatur and Wise Country.

Then the scope of my activities increased as more and more demands were made on me. I began conducting revivals and appearing as a guest preacher in churches in Dallas, Fort Worth, Chico, Bowie, Alvord, Bridgeport, Gainesville, Weston, Wichita Falls and even across the Red River into Oklahoma.

Somehow, I managed to make passing grades in school, although some teachers began to regard me as a fly-by-night student. Other professors defended me, however, in the homiletic discussions that revolved around me as the subject. "He has brought his hoodlum traits—the walk, the talk, the manner of dressing—with him, and he is perhaps too zealous and enthusiastic," said one. "But I have no doubt that he is sincere."

There were classes where I had a chance to defend my own actions. I admitted I was enthusiastic about my work

71

for the Lord, and that perhaps I wasn't the smartest student the school ever had—but the school was dedicated to turning out preachers, wasn't it? And I was preaching.

"Maybe we need more kneeology and less theology," I suggested. "Maybe we ought to be concerned more with giving God the glory and less with giving men and schools credit."

One evening, while in Fort Worth conducting a revival, I received a telephone call from Houston. I hung up with the face of B. Porter vivid in my mind and his long-ago words echoing in my ears. The shock must have been evident for Barbara grasped my arm and said, "What is it?"

"That was Tommy's mother," I said. "Tommy is dead!"

Porter's prophecy had been grimly fulfilled. Tommy had indeed gotten into a beef once too often—in a Houston dance hall—and his opponent had shot Tommy three times. Tommy had staggered from the dance hall to die in the street.

Tommy—whatever his faults—had remained my friend to the last, his mother said. He had often inquired about me, and she had called to tell me of his death, for she felt Tommy would have wanted me to know.

The news of Tommy's violent end haunted me for days. I had sought to dissuade him from his life of crime, but had I tried hard enough? Had I exhausted every effort? Was I in part guilty of his murder?

I did not know the answers to those questions and I fretted. But my resolve to help kids like Tommy was renewed. I began preaching in the beer halls and pool halls of Wise, Tarrant and Dallas counties, and I began accepting more and more revival engagements.

I thought of Tommy often during my two years at Decatur—which is a junior college—and afterwards, when I had transferred to Baylor University to complete my theological studies.

## "Moses in the Lion's Den!"

In all, I spent two years at Baylor; but my tenure there was staggered, and I never did get a degree because God kept calling me from my books—to revivals in Oklahoma, Kansas, Arkansas, and states as far away as New Jersey.

In Waco itself, where Baylor is situated, I held a dozen revivals. At one of these, some 500 people were converted, among them a young man whose life the Lord chose to intermingle with mine—Jerry Barnard.

Baptist publications—and the daily newspapers of Texas and elsewhere—were taking increasing note of my activities on behalf of God.

One afternoon, in answer to one of 500 revival invitations, I boarded a plane at Waco's airport and was borne aloft, bound for a large Midwestern city. The plane passed over the campus, and as I looked down from my great altitude, I saw the school drenched in sunlight and the students scattering like colorful ants—and I thought of Tommy.

I thought of the Tommy I'd known and all the Tommys that I didn't know but who existed, in that vague and lawless land within a land—the underworld.

And I knew my college days were ended.

# 5
# Half-Hoodlum, Half-Preacher

"ANY COWARD CAN FIGHT A BATTLE
WHEN HE'S SURE OF WINNING; BUT
GIVE ME THE MAN WHO HAS PLUCK
TO FIGHT WHEN HE'S SURE OF LOSING.
THAT'S MY WAY, SIR; AND THERE ARE
MANY VICTORIES WORSE THAN DEFEAT."
—"JANET'S REPENTANCE," GEORGE ELIOT

He was a big man, physically and financially—and in the eyes of the congregation of his church, to which he contributed heavily and attended regularly. He grasped my hand firmly at the conclusion of my sermon.

"Son," he boomed, "you could be the nation's leading evangelist—perhaps the world's greatest—if you would quit associating with those delinquents, dope addicts, hoodlums and human derelicts with whom you insist on mingling."

Those around us nodded assent to the wisdom of his words.

I had looked forward to meeting this man. He had figured prominently in a dream I had—the establishment of a Christian rehabilitation center for young dope addicts and hoodlums.

It was disappointing to learn that this man of affluence and influence was so narrow in his views. I mentally crossed his name off the list of people to whom I proposed to appeal for help in my project as I answered, "I'm sorry, Sir, but the Lord gave me this burden. Man, I've got to carry it!"

I watched the enthusiasm fade from his features, replaced

by cool disinterest. He was prepared to contribute generously to any evangelical endeavor that adhered to his rules —preach in the churches, to respectable people.

He probably wouldn't have demurred at financing a mission in the jungles of Africa or Asia. But he wasn't about to spend a dime to redeem a hustling girl or a hophead. Such people, in his eyes, weren't worth saving—despite the fact that the last person to whom Jesus ministered on this earth was a thief on a cross beside Him on Calvary.

There are many like this man in the church. To these people, I will always be half-hoodlum, and there will always be in their minds the suspicion that I'm trying to beat them for something. And I am—their love.

There was a time when I was prepared to compromise with this segment of the church. When I left Baylor to become a full-time evangelist, I settled my family in Dallas. The booming North Texas metropolis offered airline service to almost any part of the nation and my schedule—a revival in Memphis today, one in Miami tomorrow—made air transport a necessity. I depended upon freewill love offerings to finance all my traveling and living expenses, which were considerable since I was appearing at rallies, revivals and youth conferences all over the country.

The offerings were more than adequate for my needs and the needs of my family, so I gave the excess funds to those who needed a break. I bought them clothes, paid their rent, bought food for their babies, even financed their tuition to Bible schools and colleges. I never turned away anyone who came to me for help, even when I felt he or she might beat me. My personal feelings were that if I retrieved one of them for Christ, it was worth every dollar. For what price is the human soul?

I began, however, to draw criticism for using what many considered church funds for a "crusade among teen-age hoodlums," and at the time Barbara and I moved to Dallas, there were some who were openly attacking my practices, my appearances and my sincerity.

"What do they want of me?" I asked a pastor who told me of some of the talk.

He grinned wryly. "They want you to dress in discount clothing, live in a small house, drive a cheap car and let them approve any other expenditures you have. That's how too many people think a pastor should live."

I was still a sharp dresser and drove a flashy automobile. Barbara and I didn't have a home at the moment, although we were looking for one. We found it a week later. A home builder, a member of a Dallas church where I was then conducting a revival, offered us a new home in a subdivision in which he had an interest.

"You can have the home at cost, Pastor, less than cost really," said the man. "I think you'll like it."

Some members of the congregation drove us out to see the house. Barbara was ecstatic. It was a beautiful home, far more spacious and lovely than we'd ever known and, I had to admit, a rare bargain at the price asked—a gift of the builder's heart, really.

I told Barbara and the congregation members that we'd have to turn down the builder's offer.

"We couldn't live in a house like this," I argued. "We got enough people bum-rapping us as it is. They'd really be down on us if we moved into this place."

Barbara was crestfallen and the laymen were aghast, but I was adamant. I wasn't going to give my detractors any more ammunition.

I reckoned without Dallas ingenuity and obstinacy. The next week, the group of laymen approached me and handed me a sheaf of papers—the deed to the home, the insurance papers and a mortgage payment book, all in my name.

"We prayed some on this, Brother," drawled the spokesman. "And if a prizefighter can live in a $50,000 house and

Hollywood stars can throw wild parties in million-dollar mansions, why, a preacher can have something nice, too. The Lord didn't intend for his pastors to be paupers!"

Barbara and I spent the next two weeks moving into our lovely home and furnishing it.

One of our first house guests was a dope addict. His name was Fat Boy. The Dallas police had busted him for "investigation," a word that covers a multitude of sins in police lexicons. A minister who had visited the jail the day Fat Boy was arrested brought me the message that Fat Boy wanted to see me.

"He says he's a friend of yours," said the minister dubiously.

"He is," I replied. Fat Boy was my age. He was from Houston's North Side; and, like me, Fat Boy was a product of the Black Shirts. I drove at once to the jail, where I was becoming well-known, and a guard escorted me to Fat Boy's cell.

He was dirty, unshaven and needed a haircut. He was also low and on the verge of the cold turkey jitters. When he saw me, he reached through the spaces between the cell door bars and grabbed me.

Junkies are the smoothest con artists in the world. A carnival grifter has nothing on a dope fiend. When a junkie is putting down a story, not even another hophead can separate all the wheat from the chaff.

"I've had it, Cat," Fat Boy said in low, flat tones. "I'm ready to pull up and square up. I was told you'd help me."

I wasn't really listening to Fat Boy's words. I was listening to his eyes. They mirrored a dismal desperateness and the pain of a man with a grease burn on his soul.

I got him out of jail. I took him to a barbershop and paid for a haircut and a shave. I took him to a men's shop and bought him some new clothes. And then I took him home.

Ordinarily, I would have staked him to a week's room rent and money to pay for food and miscellaneous items, and I would have checked on him daily; but Fat Boy was in such a state of depression that I decided to abandon my usual procedures. I was afraid he'd take his life unless watched closely.

"What kind of habit you got?" I asked.

"I ain't real strung out, but it's more'n a yen," Fat Boy replied.

"Where's your equipment?" Junkies generally carry part or all of their own "works"—the bent spoon, hypodermic needle, eyedropper, etc.—which are the necessary paraphernalia for taking drugs intravenously. It is hidden except when in use.

Fat Boy shook his head. "I didn't bring up a spike or nothin'. I been usin' another cat's works."

I drew the car over to the curb and looked at Fat Boy. "I'm going to buy your story, Fat Boy. But you got to go all the way, or I ain't going to fool with you ever again—hear?"

"I ain't playin' no angle, Cat," Fat Boy said wearily. "I ain't going to split on you."

Babs was not surprised when I told her that Fat Boy would be staying with us for a few days. I suppose from the first she had known it would be only a matter of time until our home became a sort of "half-way house" for hoods.

She made Fat Boy welcome. And she nursed him through the "cold turkey" period of withdrawal. Fat Boy really hadn't been hooked too badly on junk, for he had no real bad pain. Within a week he was accompanying me to revival meetings; and on the third day thereafter, he made a decision for Christ.

That night he asked me and Babs if we'd help him with another problem. His wife and daughter were still in Houston, where the woman worked as a prostitute—an occupation she followed to support her own dope habit, not her baby. I remembered her as a Cottage Grove deb, a former gang girl.

I arranged for a friend in Houston to locate Fat Boy's wife and child and put them on the train for Dallas. Fat Boy, Babs and I met her at the station.

She looked pleasantly surprised when she saw Fat Boy (who never had been fat) in his new clothes and new manners, but her voice was cynical. "You look cool, Honey. How many tricks you got lined up for me?"

Fat Boy winced. She'd been a gang girl when he'd married her—and certainly no virgin—but it was he who'd turned her out as a whore.

For a week Fat Boy's wife remained bitterly skeptical concerning his conversion, during which time she went through a painful withdrawal from her drug habit. But one night, during the altar call at the conclusion of services at the church where I was appearing, I looked down into her face; and she was smiling through tears. "If Fat Boy's going to walk the Jesus road, then so am I," she sniffled.

Six months later Fat Boy left Texas for Louisiana and a good job as an electrician, taking with him a happy wife and a child who will grow up in a decent, Christian home. I know, for I've watched that child grow for almost 10 years now, and I visit Fat Boy and his wife whenever I'm in their state.

There are many who followed Fat Boy: Jackie Boy and his wife; Billy and Bobby; Paul and Willie; Bubba and Eloise; Larry and Frank; Glenn and Gerald, and a host of others whose names have larded many a prayer.

They came singly or by twos and threes, and they came at all hours of the day and night. Some of them came just to work an angle—and I'll admit that not a few of them beat me. But most of them came because something inside them cried out in protest against the life they were leading, and anything—even a "Jesus kick"—was better than what they had.

Some of them found a better life, and left to become hard-working, honest, God-fearing citizens; some left to serve God as preachers, as missionaries and as witnesses to His glory, but too many of them left to die of an overdose of heroin or goofballs, to be cut down by the gun of a cop or a companion or to go back to the streets and eventually to prison.

One day Babs and I left, too. We returned to Houston to make it the base of the newly incorporated "Freddie Gage Evangelistic Association," a non-profit organization composed of Christian businessmen and professional men and church leaders who agreed to govern my financial affairs. I was placed on a salary, and any expenditures I made beyond that salary had to be approved by the board of directors. The move effectively silenced any who still complained of my handling of the money given me.

Babs and I had to sell our beautiful home in Dallas, and we did so at a profit. I offered the money over and above what I had in the house to the builder, but he refused to take it.

"It doesn't seem right that I should profit by your generosity," I protested.

The builder smiled. "I figure the Lord and me both made a profit from that house, son."

Actually, except for the inconvenience of moving our household goods and locating a suitable house in Houston, there was no interruption of either my evangelistic work or my ministry amidst the underworld. I didn't miss a single out-of-state evangelistic engagement; and before the dishes were unpacked in our new home, hoodlums, prostitutes and dope fiends were ringing on the telephone. They were seeking spiritual counsel, just plain advice, food, lodging or money for their "monkey" or their "mouthpiece."

# Pulpit in the Shadows

In the years I'd been away from Houston—according to what I read in the newspapers—I'd matured as a person and as an evangelist, and had expanded my knowledge, theologically, sociologically and academically.

"Gone are the hoodlum manners," commented one religious writer, perhaps with more hope than conviction. He really should have waited a few weeks before offering any editorial observations.

My first month back in Houston, I accepted an invitation to speak to the congregation of a large, new Baptist church —a "harbinger of a new and greater North Side"—just off the "Bloody Burma Road." The pastor was an austere, gaunt-cheeked man who obviously didn't approve of his board of deacons' invitation to me to be a guest speaker in his pulpit.

"I'm afraid you'll find us lacking in hoodlums, Reverend," the pastor told me thinly. "It has been my experience that they just don't come to church."

"Did you ever try going out and inviting them?" I asked in reply. It wasn't the most auspicious thing that I could have said.

The hoodlums came to church that night without invitation. They came to harass me.

There were seven of them, all young toughs with ducktail haircuts, pegged pants, pointed-toed shoes and a marijuana sheen to their eyes. They swaggered down the aisle in the midst of the regular pastor's preliminary sermon and sprawled into a pew, laughing and snapping their fingers. They ignored an usher's admonition and grabbed songbooks from the racks on the back of the pew in front of them, leafing through the pages, whistling and dropping the books.

The pastor's voice rose in an attempt to override their babble and then faltered. His face began to redden and members of the congregation around the hoodlums began to stir nervously. One of the boys began to clean his nails with a long-bladed knife.

I was off my chair behind the pulpit and down the aisle before I thought. I dropped my Bible into the lap of a woman and grabbed the boy with the knife.

"Give me that shiv, you little sprout!" I spat, twisting the knife from his hand and pulling him out of his seat.

"Who do you punks think you are? This is God's house—not a pool hall. Do you think you can come in here and rouse the Lord's people like they're a bunch of sprouts? Not while I'm around. I'll hook it up with you in a minute, and if you don't believe it, let's go outside and get it on! Now you characters better snap or get with it!"

I started peeling my coat.

The kids snapped. The one I had yanked from his seat threw his hands up, and the bravado in his voice was replaced by a quaver when he squawked, "No, preacher, no! We were just kiddin' around!"

"You come to the House of God and commit blasphemy—and you call it kiddin' around?" I roared.

"Now, sit down, all of you, and keep quiet! You came to church, and you're going to stay until church is out!"

I preached my sermon that night to those kids, and I don't know to this day who was the more shocked, frightened and discomfited—the seven young hoods or the turtle-shelled pastor.

There are a lot of pastors like him, living within a protective shell where, with their minds geared to impressing their congregation, they lose sight of the world and its realities. They preach the "positive Gospel," all good things, and ignore the "negative" things such as addiction, poverty, alcoholism, juvenile delinquency and the other miseries of life. Some of these pastors don't realize that they are loafing on the Lord's time.

## Pulpit in the Shadows

I conducted a revival near Galveston once, when that island city on the Gulf of Mexico was the sin center of the Lone Star State. The city's gambling halls, bordellos, dope dens and flesh pots ran wide open around the clock—tolerated and ignored, by and large, by the citizenry and ministry.

The general philosophy was that a controlled and regulated vice system was economically healthy—attracting, as it did, hordes of tourists and others looking for "action." Only a few cried out that such an economy was a tainted one, based on the exploitation of human values and lives. And oddly enough, those few were mostly businessmen and middle class citizens, with only a handful of preachers among them.

The church in which I conducted this particular revival was in a lovely residential section. The pastor was older than I, but still young, and very much impressed with his congregation which was composed of the community's wealthier and more influential men and their families. He was strictly a "square John," and an obvious look of relief lighted his face when he met me and saw that I didn't have a stick of weed tucked over one ear or a shiv in my belt and that I didn't talk out of the side of my mouth.

"After the service, we're having dinner with Mr. So-and-So," he said, trying to use the name casually. I recognized it, as anyone who glances at a newspaper once a week would. Actually, I had met the tycoon before, although I didn't mention it.

There were two men at the services that night who were not wealthy or influential. I spotted them in a back row midway through the services—two junkies who looked like they were both strained out. I knew them both, and I knew that they had to be up tight to seek me out in church.

When I sought them out after services, I found that they

86

were in trouble, and that they were high on heroin. I excused myself to the pastor—who had stayed at my elbow since the services ended—and took the boys into the vestry. You do not solve problems such as they had in a few hours, or even a few months, so I was not with them long—no longer than was necessary to set up a schedule of visits with them in my home in Houston.

When I rejoined the pastor, he was visibly nettled. He nodded toward the rich man and his wife in the lobby.

"Don't you think that was rude?" he snapped. "Holding up these people while you talked to those two boys. They've no business here!"

I flipped my lid.

"Who has better business here than those in need of God!" I blazed. "If I didn't have any more compassion than you, I'd get out of the ministry. You're worried about the feelings of an 'up-and-outer' man who wants to buy you dinner. Well, Pastor, you go eat dinner with that man. But if you've got any guts, you'll skip that dinner and come with me!"

My tirade stunned him, and then his amazement gave way to abashment, which in turn gave way to curiosity. My challenge intrigued him. He suddenly smiled and nodded.

"You're right, of course. I'm the rude one. Let me tell Mr. So-and-So we can't join him and I'll be right with you."

Less than five minutes later, we were in my car.

"Where are we going?" the pastor asked.

I put the car in gear and eased into the stream of traffic before I answered.

"I'm going to show you some people Jesus died for," I said.

I drove to Post Office Street, at that time one of the most infamous avenues in the world. Behind the gay curtains and bright blinds that masked the windows of the brownstone, brick and frame buildings on each side of the street, an untold number of lives had been blighted, an untold number of dreams had died. Inside those houses there was laughter and there was pleasure, but it was hollow laughter and a deadly pleasure.

There were several teen-age kids drinking and carousing in a car in front of the house where I stopped. My companion eyed the house curiously as we stepped up the flight of three steps. I rang the doorbell.

"What is this?" he asked.

I looked at him, startled. He really didn't know!

"This is a house of ill-repute, a house of prostitution—a cathouse, as they'd say in certain circles."

He was shocked. Disbelief was written all over his features, but it banished when the door opened. There stood a saucy-faced girl in a red cocktail dress that had all the elements of temptation in either its design or its wearing—I really couldn't tell which. The pastor beside me gasped.

"What's the happenin's," I drawled.

She swung the door wider and smiled wantonly. "Come on in, baby, and find out."

The pastor jumped backwards. He was scared to death, and refused to go inside when I asked him if he'd like to meet some of the girls. I turned back to the girl and handed her a Gospel tract.

"Thank you—and God bless you," I said. She looked at the tract and closed the door in my face—but not before I saw the shame that flooded her features.

As we were walking back to my car, two men were getting out of a cab in front of the place. By their dress and their appearance, they might have just come from church.

We visited a score of taverns, gambling joints and dives that afternoon. We drank cokes and passed out tracts and talked to perverts, prostitutes, dope addicts, pimps, drunkards and others who frequented the places we entered. When we ended the tour, my friend wore a somber, brooding and hurt expression—the look worn by soldiers coming out of the battle line, doctors emerging from surgery where they have just lost a patient and people who have just undergone a shattering experience.

"I knew it existed, of course," he commented with a sigh. "But I'd never been out in it—it did not concern me."

He was silent for a short time, and then he turned to me and exclaimed, "But Freddie, we can't save everyone!"

I nodded. "No, we can't save everyone. But we can try to save some—even one."

I didn't see him for several weeks. When I did, he grasped my hand and hugged me to him. He did not look the same. He glowed with warmth, compassion and enthusiasm for the Lord.

"You have changed my whole ministry, Freddie," he said excitedly. "And you've changed the lives of some of my congregation, too. We go forth to evangelize now, down where the people in need are—out on the streets. I don't know how much good we're doing those people, but I do know the good they're doing us! We feel like we're really working for God now!"

I wish I could say there are many pastors like him, but I can't. Of the 100 or so that I have persuaded to accompany me on such safaris into the jungles of sin, only 35 or 40 have been affected by their experiences. The others were only disgusted by what they saw—and annoyed at me for exposing them to dirt and degradation. They were glad to return to the shelter of their little worlds, where the most serious problems facing them were attendance in Sunday school, the annual picnic and how much they could raise this year to send missionaries to Africa.

This is something I will never understand, I guess. Why

do we send so many missionaries to Africa, Asia and India when we've got nearly as many savages in our own jungles who need saving?

I think it proves a point made to me once: The Church is the only business in the whole world that can be *in* business, and yet be *out* of business without going out of business!

# 6
# Requiem for Sonny

"THERE IS SO MUCH GOOD IN THE WORST OF US,
AND SO MUCH BAD IN THE BEST OF US,
THAT IT ILL BEHOOVES ANY OF US
TO FIND FAULT WITH THE REST OF US."

—ANONYMOUS

The sonic searching of the telephone shredded the silk cocoon of sleep, and I looked into the luminescent face of the clock as I lifted the receiver. It was 5:30 A.M., June 27, 1961.

"Hello."

What vapors of sleep still clouded my senses fled before the anguished voice in my ear. "Freddie—Sonny's been shot, and he's dying! He's asking for you!"

"I'll be right there," I replied, mechanically noting the name of the hospital and the room number; but it wasn't until I was in my car, driving through the soft dawn, that my heart accepted the message. Sonny was dying! And as I acknowledged the dismal fact, I thought of a passage from the Scriptures, I John 5:16:

If any man see his brother sin a sin which is not unto death, he shall ask, and he shall give him life for them that sin not unto death.
There is a sin unto death: I do not say that he should pray for it.

The verse flitted across the marquee of my mind all the way to the hospital. I could not suppress it, even as I stepped from the elevator and hurried down the corridor toward Sonny's room. A group of people were clustered near a window at the end of the hallway, and I recognized Sonny's mother and sister among them. There were two other girls a pace apart from this group, and while I did not know either of them, I catalogued them instantly—call girls.

I knew, too, that I had not arrived in time, as Sonny's mother turned her misery-brimmed face. "He's dead, Freddie," she said dully. "They just took his body away."

I took her hand, unable to speak. I could not comfort her, for rising in me were a thousand remembrances of her son and the painful awareness of my own role in Sonny's destruction. I did not then know the name of the man who had fired the bullets into Sonny's body, but his regret could be no more than mine.

Perhaps Sonny's mother sensed the remorseful memories that flogged me, for she squeezed my hand and said, "Don't, Freddie. It was none of your doing. He would have told you that himself. His last words to me were about you. He said that he knew he'd led a sorry life and wanted to make up for it. He told me, 'I don't think I'll make it, but if I do, Mother, I will turn to God and you and I will work together for the Lord.' I want you to see to his funeral, Freddie. I want you to conduct the services."

I promised I would and left, and still in my mind was the thought: There was a sin unto death, and Sonny had sinned that sin.

Somewhere between the hospital and my home, when I stopped at a red light, I became aware that a woman in the car beside mine was staring at me. It was then that I realized I was sobbing. I cried all the way home.

When I arrived, a reporter was waiting. Somehow he had learned that Sonny and I had been close in the past. He was also aware of Sonny's former prominence as an athlete and of the promising career that had loomed for him. "What happened, Reverend?" the newsman asked. I don't think he really sought an answer, but I gave him one.

"Sonny got in with the wrong crowd," I said bleakly.

The reporter nodded. He didn't ask me what "wrong crowd." I would have answered that question, too—my crowd.

Sonny's death was bannered in the headlines. One line of bold type asked: WHAT CAUSED PROMISING CAREER TO GO SOUR?

I had asked myself that same question many times, before Sonny was gunned down. In the days following his death, I reviewed our association, seeking the answer to another question: What was my own share of guilt in Sonny's death?

From the moment I surrendered to a call to preach the Gospel of Christ, Sonny's salvation had been one of my personal goals. I not only wanted him to accept Christ, I wanted Sonny to preach the glory of the Lord.

I still feel that Sonny would have been a wonderful spokesman for God. Even in the days when I was a companion in sin and carnality, I'd never regarded Sonny as a full-fledged hoodlum. I'd analyzed Sonny, with a street tough's insight (or was it instinct?), as a man who wandered a Pavlov's maze of desires, trapped between goodness and badness—and never able to associate himself wholly with either. I saw him as just "half hep."

Sonny was one of those who had sincerely delighted in my conversion. And shortly afterward, in that year of 1951, he had disassociated himself with the underworld and accepted a scholarship to the University of Houston. His disassociation, however, lasted less than six months. I learned of his regression when I entered a tavern to preach one afternoon and found Sonny entertaining a group of prostitutes, pimps and thieves.

95

"Why did you quit the university, Sonny?" I asked in surprise. Sonny lifted his shoulders.

"I didn't fit," he replied casually.

Several days later, speaking to a high school assembly, I spotted Sonny in the audience, but when I looked for him afterwards, he was gone. Thereafter, Sonny appeared at dozens of the revivals that I conducted in Houston and surrounding cities. Sometimes he would stay and we would talk afterwards, but more often he disappeared immediately after my sermon.

At each of these revivals, I singled Sonny out with my eyes when I implored those who had not accepted Christ as their Savior to come to the altar, and several times I left the pulpit to plead with him face to face.

Sonny, each time, shook his head adamantly. "But don't worry, Cat, you'll get me yet," he laughed once.

"I don't want you—Christ does," I smiled in reply.

I had a feeling that Sonny wanted Christ. I know he was searching for something that would meet an inner need. I could see the yearning in his eyes at times and sense the longing in his voice, and I tried to convince him that his want and his need were one and the same—Christ.

Sonny scoffed at me. "That's okay for you, kid. But you ain't talking about me. What I want, I'll get. What I need, I'll find."

That year Barbara bore me a son (the first of four) and we named him Daniel—after Dan Vestal. That same year, Sonny was married to a lovely Christian girl, and both Barbara and I came to know and love Dottie. "Maybe she'll straighten him out, like you did me," I joshed Barbara.

Barby smiled, a little sadly, and shook her head.

"I didn't straighten you out," she said. "I tried, but I couldn't. God straightened you out."

I put my arms around her and kissed her. "Yeah, I guess

96

He did. But He had a lot of help from you, and maybe He'll get some help from Dottie."

Shortly after Barbara and I had moved to Decatur and I had entered the Baptist college, I heard that Sonny had enrolled at Baylor. Barbara and I were elated, as much for Dottie's sake as for Sonny's. I felt that if Sonny stuck it out at Baylor, got a degree and went on to provide his family a decent way of life, he could do nothing less, sooner or later, than accept Christ.

Baylor, however, palled on Sonny within a few months. When next we heard of him, he was back in Houston and was accumulating a police record as a brawler and a hoodlum.

The tempo of my evangelistic work increased steadily; and I began to travel more and more, preaching the Gospel in small hamlets, in big cities, in rural crossroads—wherever the hand of God directed me—but I never wholly lost contact with Sonny. When I would preach to prisoners in jails and in penitentiaries, his name would sometimes crop up; and there were times when kids, hooked on dope or sick of the hoodlum life, would seek me out and say, "Sonny said to look you up—you'd help me." Sometimes Sonny would call me (usually when he was in trouble or of a troubled mind) or would write me.

When we were not in close contact—sometimes for periods of months on end—the grapevine kept each of us informed of the other's activities.

The grapevine informed Sonny of my growing repute as a preacher. And the grapevine posted me on Sonny's growing reputation as a procurer.

He had completely submerged himself in vice and was regarded as one of the key figures in Houston call girl activities. He drove a Cadillac, sported diamond rings and stickpins and carried a thick roll of bills—the hallmarks of success shared by pimps and petroleum magnates in the great Southwest. The single grain of solace gleaned from the reports on Sonny was the fact that Dottie remained untainted by his activities.

"They got a kid, and she's always after Sonny to pull up on account of the kid, but he won't," one hoodlum told me.

Sonny's seeming defection to evil not only bitterly disappointed and saddened me, but it created in me a guilt complex. I could not forget that I had given Sonny the first stick of weed he'd ever smoked, and I could not know how much of the wild crop Sonny was cultivating was due to the seeds I had sown. Barbara disagreed with this viewpoint.

"I like Sonny, too, and I wanted as much as you to see him saved," she argued. "But Sonny was doing bad things when he met you, and he knew all about marijuana. If he hadn't gotten it from you, he'd have gotten it somewhere else. You've done more good for Sonny than bad!"

Barby's was perhaps a valid rationale, but I was never able to accept it.

Sonny was a burden I took to Christ in prayer uncounted times, and in due time the Lord shared the burden.

I visited Houston several months later, to conduct a revival on the North Side. As usual, I accepted several other invitations to speak to school student bodies and to other church groups, jamming these engagements into an already full schedule; and I had little time for sleep.

Barbara and I were billeted in the parsonage of the church where I was conducting the revival, and I was lying across the bed one afternoon when the pastor of the church knocked on the door and entered.

"There is someone here to see you, Freddie," he said. "I told him you were resting, and I'll send him away if you like."

I sat up and shook my head. "No, tell him to come in." I

stepped to the wash basin and splashed some cold water on my face.

When I turned, Sonny was standing in the doorway.

We eyed each other silently for a moment—a pastor and a panderer whose lives were curiously intermingled—and then Sonny stepped into the room, walking a little stiffly.

"How's it going, Reverend," Sonny said softly and grabbed me by the shoulders in the affectionate way he had.

He looked sharp. His clothes were obviously from the best shops, and he gave the appearance of the wealthy, well-groomed man who has reason to be proud of himself. But a faint patina of decadence overlaid Sonny's handsome features, and the shadow of despair clouded his irises.

"I'm glad to see you, Sonny," I said, and slapped him lightly on the side. I felt the bandages beneath his clothes, and he winced at my touch. "What's the matter?" I asked, alarmed.

Sonny recovered with a smile. "Aw, I got into a beef with a boy, and he cut me up a little. Don't worry about it."

He sat down and we talked, of inconsequential things at first, sparring with words like two fighters seeking an opening. I sensed that Sonny was not here to pass a few minutes with a special friend, as had been the case in the past when he called on me. Finally, I asked, "What are you doing these days, Sonny?" I knew the answer, and Sonny knew I knew.

His grin was defiant, but shame tinged his one-word reply. "Playing."

I nodded, keeping his eyes locked with mine. "If you play, Sonny, you have to pay—you know that," I said.

Sonny's lips curled in a wry grimace and he stood up and began pacing, spurred by his thoughts. Then he stopped and faced me.

"That's right, kid—I know that. That's why I'm here! I told you you'd get me one day, and this is the day. I don't like this life I've got. It's a lousy life. I've got a lot of money, but it's dirty money. Every dollar of it is marked by a girl's shame—there's not a clean penny in my pocket.

"I don't want that kind of life anymore, Cat. I got a square wife and a baby, and all I've brought them is shame. I want to change my life, Freddie—I want to accept Christ!"

Sonny was sincere! I realized this as I looked at him, his face afire with determination, and a tidal wave of happiness washed over me.

"Hallelujah!" I shouted, bringing the startled pastor to the door; and he stood there, amazed and smiling, as Sonny and I hugged each other and shouted. Then we all three knelt down and gave thanks to God for Sonny's deliverance.

Sonny stayed for supper with us, and then he stayed for church; and that night will live in my memory on the other side of eternity.

There were more than 1,250 people at that service, and when I gave the altar call, Sonny marched down the aisle and stepped to the pulpit himself.

"Freddie Gage turned me out," he said, looking at me with his brilliant smile. "But tonight he's turning me in—to Jesus Christ!"

Of all the revivals I have conducted, that particular one remains one of the most memorable. Word of Sonny's conversion, as had word of mine, swept the city like a prairie fire. The next night over 1,700 persons attended the services. The church could not seat them all, so we borrowed chairs and seated the overflow on the lawn. It was a situation we learned to cope with during the tenure of the revival.

Scores of young hoodlums followed Sonny's example. They trooped down the aisle nightly, and in the morning we'd find trace chains, cans of beer, switchblades, brass knucks, slapsticks and other such paraphernalia beside the church steps or tossed in the hedges.

## Requiem for Sonny

One morning the pastor found a small bag with some tobacco-like substance inside. "What's this?" he asked, looking puzzled.

I needed only to look. "That's tea," I said dryly.

"Really!" exclaimed the pastor, sniffing at the contents of the bag. "It doesn't smell like any tea I've ever known."

"It's marijuana—dope!" I explained. Later that day I turned the weed over to a narcotics officer.

Two or three nights before the revival ended, Sonny sought me out at the conclusion of a service. "Where do we go from here, Cat?" he asked, smiling.

"Texarkana," I replied. "But what's this 'we' business?"

Sonny's brow furrowed. "Why, I thought I was going with you. I thought we'd be a team. Man, the only way I can make it is to get out of town."

During the first year of my ministry to the underworld, I had learned that the most difficult problem involved was not winning the hoodlum to Christ, but holding him. It was my job to win them. It was up to the local pastors to hold them. And therein was the crux of the problem. Perhaps theirs was the more difficult of the two tasks—I do not know. I do know that too many pastors wanted all the outlaws saved, but very few of them wanted these converted criminals in their churches.

Those who did accept the saved hoodlums wanted to put them on five years of spiritual probation. What it amounted to, really, was that the pastors wanted these hoodlums to accept Christ, and to believe that belief in the Saviour washed them white as snow, but the pastors themselves didn't have too much faith in the bleaching process.

Faced with this attitude, and ostracized in other ways by other members of the congregation, too many converts returned to their old ways and old associates.

Many of the dope fiends and thieves whom I persuaded to

make a decision sensed the rocky climb ahead of them. Most of them begged to accompany me on my evangelical circuit. I had to refuse them. I had to refuse Sonny, too.

"Man, I can't take along everybody that wants to go with me," I tried to explain. "If I did, I'd soon have thousands trooping along, and pretty soon there'd be hundreds of them just along for the ride. It's not easy to be a Christian, Sonny. I never told you it would be, but you're one man I know can make it."

Before I left I went to a religious bookstore and bought a Bible. I had Sonny's name stamped on the leather cover in gold. On the flyleaf I wrote: "This Bible will keep you away from sin. Sin will keep you away from this Bible."

I presented the Bible to Sonny on the last night of the revival. He cried and begged again to go with me, but I referred him to Phillipians 4:13: "I can do all things through Christ which strengtheneth me."

I prayed for Sonny all the way to Texarkana, recalling how Dan Vestal had done the same for me, and when I was settled in my hotel room I wrote Sonny a letter.

Two days later, Sonny called me. Temptation was already tugging at him. His former companions were giving him a tough go. "I'm in a switch, kid," Sonny pleaded. "I don't know if I can make it or not. Lemme come up there!"

I demurred. "I can't be your backbone, Sonny. You're supposed to be making it for Christ, not me. You get in with a Christian crowd, and you'll make it. You hear?"

Sonny laughed. It was his old laugh, clear and confident. "Okay, Cat—I hear."

I wrote him often. I also wrote Paul Carlin, who was preaching in Houston at the time, and asked him to lend his strength and faith to Sonny's fight. Paul, like me, had known Sonny in the old days. Paul promised to do what he could, although he was about to go on an evangelical circuit himself.

102

# Requiem for Sonny

Several months passed before I returned to Houston. I had not heard from Sonny during the last several weeks of that time.

As soon as I arrived in Houston, I hurried to his home and pounded on the door. Sonny admitted me. There were several others in the apartment. I recognized all of them as characters. Wine, whiskey and beer bottles littered the room; and the acrid odor of weed permeated the place.

I looked at Sonny, who returned my stare with a dispassionate air.

"Why, Sonny? Why?"

His voice was cool. "I didn't fit."

"Where's Dottie?"

A spark glowed briefly in the depths of his eyes. "She cut out. Took the kid with her. You'd better cut out, too, Reverend."

"Yes," I sighed. "I guess I had."

It was not our last contact with each other. I saw Sonny frequently over the years, and occcasionally I would spot him in the crowd at revivals that I conducted. Each time I saw him, I pleaded with him to return to Christ. Each time Sonny rejected my entreaties. I had the eerie feeling that we were on a mystical merry-go-round.

I suppose there are degrees of goodness and badness. Sonny was a "good" pimp, I have been told. That meant he was not bad to the girls he controlled. He treated them fairly, allowing them to keep a generous share of their earnings. He did not beat them, and he attempted to steer them clear of narcotics. His girls adored him. Sonny was a highly successful "Big Daddy."

As an actual husband and father, Sonny was a total failure. Dottie divorced Sonny, and he married one of his call girls. That girl also divorced him, and Sonny persuaded Dottie to remarry him. She bore him two more children before their final separation. I did not see Dottie too often during those years. I could only guess at the ordeal to which she was being subjected by the shame and despair in her face.

Sonny's disintegration was more marked. Each time I saw him his eyes would be duller, his features more puffed. The crucible of vice was melting all the fine metal that was in him.

Paradoxically, Sonny continued to send troubled hoodlums and debs to me, and many were converted to Christianity and a purposeful life. In fact, it was in connection with a prostitute's plight that I last talked to Sonny on the night of June 25, 1961. The girl was a dope fiend and she had a small baby. She could not care for her burning habit and her baby, too, so she wanted to give the baby away.

"She ain't one of my girls," Sonny explained. "She's just a kid who needs help. I thought of you right away, Reverend. You'll take the kid and give it a home, won't you?"

"No," I replied. "You just don't handle unwanted children like that. But if you'll bring the girl and her baby to my home tomorrow, I will be able to advise her on the proper steps to take to place her child up for adoption."

"That's good enough for me," Sonny drawled. "See you right after breakfast, Cat."

He didn't. Why Sonny didn't keep the appointment, I don't know. I only know that less than 24 hours later Sonny was shot down in front of a motel on the "Bloody Burma Road."

When I read the stories of the incident, I noted that Sonny's killer was an old acquaintance. Police described the tragedy as a "drunken fight over a woman."

The only eyewitness, a businessman who did not know either Sonny or his killer, corroborated the police theory. In his written statement to police, the man said he was at the motel to see a salesman. He said he did not know either man involved in the shooting, except as they had been identified to him by police. He had seen both Sonny and the other man earlier in the motel bar.

"I was leaving and was outside when Sonny drove up and asked me to tell B.J. to come out and talk. They had an argument earlier about a girl named Lucille. . . . B.J. came out and Sonny asked to shake hands. B.J. turned and started walking away. Then Sonny jumped out of the car and started hitting B.J. with a shotgun. B.J. pulled a revolver from inside his coat and fired four times. One shot nicked me in the arm. . . ."

The chapel where Sonny's funeral was held was packed for the occasion. It was a motley congregation, as I noted from the pulpit above the coffin. There were safecrackers, gunmen, panderers, dope addicts, prostitutes, detectives, teachers, student athletes and professional athletes—and a few of the morbidly curious who are always found at the funerals of those who die violently.

I looked down at Sonny's waxen features, molded in the semblance of sleep by the undertaker's skill; and then I began my sermon.

"Sonny played and lost," I said. "But I am not here to pass judgment on him, for as an anonymous poet once wrote, 'There is so much good in the worst of us, and so much bad in the best of us, that it ill behooves any of us to find fault with the rest of us.'"

I told the congregation of my own association with Sonny —the impact that he had had on my life, and the possible impact that I had had on his. I spared neither myself nor Sonny, and I concluded: "I knew him at his best, and I knew him at his worst—and yet I wonder sometimes if I knew him at all?"

I lingered at the cemetery after the short services there. Sonny's grave was almost covered when I left, and in my mind was the question that I had posed myself on Sonny's death: What was my own share of guilt?

It was a question I finally asked the Lord in prayer. He answered through the U.S. mail.

Dottie was not at Sonny's funeral. I did not know what had happened to her, or to Sonny's children. But one day among my mail was a letter. I present it herewith in part:

January 25, 1965
The Reverend Freddie Gage
3312 Austin
Houston, Texas

Dear Freddie:

You and Barbara have been much on my mind lately. . . . I'm sure you had wondered what had happened to us. I was living in _____ when Sonny was killed. I had been there almost 6 months. At the time, I had not seen him for about 8 months. I had been separated from him for about a year.

After I left the last time, I never felt one regret—I knew I was through trying for both of us—and I was sick of the untold misery we were being subjected to and the children were getting old enough to see how he was treating me.

When C. . . . called me and told me he was dead of course there was the numb shock—but after many, many days, I gradually felt a great relief; relief that the children and I would not be subjected to any more misery, as he seemed to spread it to everyone he came in contact with—because he was so miserable himself. I felt, and still do feel, that God took his life. I prayed, cried, loved him through so much that I felt he wanted desperately to live for God, but would never let God take complete control of his life, so there he hung, suspended and miserable. Of course, memories of all kinds continue to plague me, and after I've been to Houston—it's as if a thick cloud of memories hang around me and it's several days before I can shake it. I know it will take me several years to set

106

my mind at complete ease about him—you just don't know Sonny and forget him and you certainly don't love him and ever forget him.

I cannot begin to explain how God has blessed us here in ————. My life is very full.

May the grace of our wonderful Lord surround you, your family and the wonderful work you have begun and may His abounding love and guidance be your daily portion.

Much love and prayers,

Dorothy

P.S.—Freddie, though I never voiced my thanks to you, I am deeply grateful for your love and prayers and patience with Sonny through all the years—he loved you very much and depended on your love. God bless you for all you did and all you wanted to do!

I will always treasure Dottie's letter. I have read it many times since receiving it. And I never finish it without knowing: There is balm in Gilead. There is a physician there.

# 7
# Roses from a Dark Garden

". . . HE THAT IS WITHOUT SIN AMONG YOU, LET HIM FIRST CAST A STONE AT HER."

—JOHN 8:7

S he was 19, a girl of vivid charm, and a "race horse" among
prostitutes. Such a hustling girl can "turn tricks right
and left," to use the descriptive phraseology of the trade.
Her kind of girl is a valuable asset to any panderer, especially one with a dope habit. And her pimp was real "strung
out."

I don't recall what brought them to church services that
afternoon—perhaps they came to see a friend, for the services were held in the chapel of Teen Liberators, a "whole
way" house for hoodlums—but I do recall that I sought
them out afterwards, for I had been trying for months to
lead the man to Christ. That afternoon, as before, he was
aloof to my entreaties and moved away after a few minutes.
The girl stayed, however.

Apparently, my suppliances had struck a chord of her
conscience, for her eyes shimmered with tears. And behind
the tears, I seemed to see a hope of heaven.

"How long have you been at this game?" I asked.

Shame flooded her face. "About a year, I guess."

111

"Wouldn't you like to quit and live a decent life—a life for Christ?" I persisted. She nodded and began to weep openly.

"Then why don't you?" I argued. "Can't you see it's not just your body you're selling—it's your soul! And for what? Everything you earn goes back into his arm. Why, girl, you're helping him to commit murder!"

Shock showed through her tears. "Murder!" she gasped. "How?"

"By selling yourself so he can buy the dope he needs," I said. "Anyone who uses dope is committing suicide on the installment plan, and what is suicide but murder of one's self."

Before I could debate the question further—and perhaps win her to salvation—her pimp grabbed her arm and pulled her away from me.

"Look, Reverend, don't mess with her," he said in a tone of voice which was meant to be jocular, but which was also fraught with both fright and anger. "She's my meal ticket, my score money! Man, she's all I got goin' for me!"

It was several more months before I saw her again. She was then a dope fiend herself. She was still attractive, but hers was now a brittle beauty, a surface loveliness that would soon be dissolved by the fire within her—the burning need for drugs.

I have known thousands of girls like her. Some (too few, I have to admit) were led to Christ through my supplications or those of associates; and when I think of the ones who were saved, my soul cries "Hallelujah!" in praise to God. But when I think of those who rejected salvation, I cry for the shameful waste of mortality. Each of the latter left a scar on my heart.

The problem of our delinquent young women is one of the most urgent facing law enforcement officials, the judiciary and sociologists today; but it is no less an insistent problem of the Church. Ministers and members who are active in church affairs can, through diligent and understanding missionary work, rescue thousands of lost girls annually. I say "rescue" because I am persuaded that the majority of girls involved in hoodlum activities—living a life of sin and degradation—are unwilling participants. I don't think I am naive in this theory. Mistaken, perhaps, but not naive.

I know from experiences during my own hoodlum years that while an ample number of girls were "volunteers," most were enticed, coerced or driven by circumstances to lives of immorality.

"I'd rather be dead than a prostitute!" one girl, a fragile blonde, cried to me. A few months later, she was dead as the result of a "hot shot," an overdose of heroin. Police theorized that an inexperienced dope peddler, who didn't know how to dilute his stuff, had sold her the fatal dosage. Perhaps this was true. And perhaps this was her way of ending it all. Too many choose the suicide route.

Few girls of the underworld can avoid the twin malignities of prostitution and dope addiction. I have known a lot of prostitutes who were not junkies. I have never known a girl with a habit who was not a prostitute. Prostitution is the cornerstone of the junkie's economy.

Female delinquents, I have noted over the years, originate at all levels of the economic structure, although girls from slum or blight environments do have an edge in numbers. Most have one thing in common: They come from non-Christian homes. Most have another thing in common, commingling with the first: They are from broken homes or homes where the parents have reneged on the responsibilities of training and discipline.

It takes little effort—only some flattering attention in too many instances—to entice such girls onto the path to destruction.

Perhaps one girl's own experiences are more illustrative

than a score of observations. Listen to A . . . . . , as her story
was recorded by me recently :

I don't know why I started taking dope. If only I
had listened. We moved here from the country. I
started to high school here. Everybody in school was
talking about kicks. They told me I ought to come by
the drugstore before school. The kids called me a
square, said I never did anything, said I was dull.

I was a square.

Some of the boys were cats. They dressed real sharp,
and all the girls went for them in a big way. They were
cool characters. They didn't notice me though, because
I was a square. Pretty soon, I got tired of being out of
things. I started skipping school. I went to the drugstore. Before long I was accepted. Instead of going to
school, we would go over to someone's pad. Usually the
parents were away. We would play bop and jazz and
dance. I started smoking. Everybody else did, and I
wanted to belong. One day, some of the characters, real
gone guys had some reefers. All of us smoked them.
We really got a bang out of them. They sure did make
a character feel high—even a square like me.

Well, it didn't take long. I learned the jive and I
learned to use the reefers. After you've tried the first
reefer, it's easy to get a yen for another. By this time, I
was having trouble with my teachers. I wasn't studying, cuttin' school all the time. I barely passed, but I
didn't care. Gosh, I was glad when summer came!

Boy, we really lived it up that summer. We stayed
out most of the nights at blast parties, made all the
nightclubs, jazz contests and all the bop joints. Every
place we went was crowded with characters.

Naturally, I slept late in the mornings. By the time
I'd get up my parents would be gone to work. The cats

would come over to my pad, and we'd have a ball. We'd really blow up the joint. We never went out in the daytime—it was too hot. Somebody would phone a connection and get our fix. Usually the pusher would say, "It's too hot. I don't want to make the deal. There's a panic on." But we had money, so he'd make a deal. I didn't have to pay because I was a hide. The boys would score for me. They would usually score for a can—that's about 70 joints (cigarettes). If stash (money) got low, I'd con my old lady for $10.00 by saying I owed it to a friend, or that I needed some hose, or anything that happened to pop into my mind at the moment.

I played it real cool at home—just the fireside type, that was me. Real cozy like. My folks never got hep. Occasionally, my old lady would ask if I had a headache or something. I guess I looked pretty rugged sometimes.

Well, I blasted the weed for over a year before I ever fixed.

One night, at a fast party, I met Danny. Danny was real sharp and handsome, too. He didn't go to school. He hung around the hot spots and pushed stuff. He was hooked.

I will never forget the first time I saw Danny take a fix. He opened a capsule of H, and carefully poured the white powder on a spoon. Then with a medicine dropper he dropped a little water on the stuff. Next he lit a match and held it under the spoon for a few seconds. Then he drew the H up into the dropper. With a hypodermic needle, he slipped it onto the dropper. I was bug-eyed by this time. I knew what he was doing, but I had never seen it before.

Danny was a mainliner. He had the monkey on his back but good.

115

He doubled up his fist and pumped until the vein popped up. Then he jabbed the needle into his vein. In a couple of seconds, it was all done. He sat down beside me on the couch. Pretty soon he was feeling high. I could see that H really did something for him. Before long, he asked me to joy-pop, said if I'd play it cool, I'd never get hooked. I said, "No." He called me a square, said he'd give me a cap free.

There they were callin' me a square again. I thought —what the heck, it won't hurt to try this once. All the other kids were doing it. They laughed at me. Oh, well, I decided to try it. Danny and I went outside. He gave me a belt and told me to wrap it around my arm. I'd seen the other kids do it, so I did what he said. When the vein popped up, Danny pushed the needle in. It hurt for a second. But in a little while after you get a fix, you don't care about anything.

You just relax, let yourself go. For a while I used Danny's needle, but soon I got one of my own. I should have known things couldn't go on like this forever.

By the time for school to start again, I was really hooked.

Danny and I decided to get married. At least that would keep me out of school. My dad hit the ceiling, said I was too young, said I had to finish school. I said we would run away and get married. That hurt them terribly. They had always counted on a church wedding for me. Daddy had counted on being able to give the bride away. Mother cried a lot. I guess she was pretty upset, too. Danny and I just wanted to get away from them. We paid no attention to what they said. As soon as we could get away from them, we got the license, hunted up a preacher and were married.

Life will really be one long ball, I thought. We rented a real cool place. All the characters came to our pad, and we really had a party. Danny supported us by selling reefers to kids and supplying H to hypes (addicts).

Pretty soon, Danny turned me out. You know, he got me dates with a few fellows who had money. Everything looked pretty good. But our luck soon ran out. Danny sold the man (a narcotics agent) and was busted. I was arrested because of the marks on my arm. It was awful. The jail was full of junkies. All I could think was, what would my family say?

Danny was out on parole when we were married, and now he'd broken it. That meant a five-year stretch in the joint. The police called my parents. They refused to believe their daughter was in jail. They said they knew the police must have made a mistake; their daughter wasn't a dope addict. It was impossible!

Dad came to the jail. When he saw me, he began to cry. I held out my "golden arm," and even Dad could read the story in the needle marks. It cost me $25.00 a day to fill that arm. That's not a real strung-out habit.

The next few days, I went through cold-turkey. It was awful. My mother said she'd rather see me dead than like I was.

I'm going to take the cure, but I wonder about it. They say only 10 percent are ever really cured. Suppose I do kick the habit, what then? Danny will be up for five years, and when he gets out, no one will give him a job. I'm not sure I can live without H. Once it gets you—well, once hooked, always hooked. Or almost. I just don't know what will happen to me now.

If only I had known what dope would do to me before I started using it!

The cry was all too familiar. The end is likely to be familiar, too. I could not persuade her that she could live without H by substituting "J"—Jesus. She is still a junkie and still a prostitute, but she no longer frets about Danny. She's hooked up with another addict.

That's how it is with dope: It dissolves first the willpower, then the morals.

The most difficult phase in weaning these girls from their wayward lives is convincing them that, in most instances, their "old man," if he's an addict, has no real affection for them. The majority of junkies have no compunctions about letting their wives or girlfriends take the rap for crimes they've committed, if they're "up tight" on the matter. It's to the credit of the police and the district attorney's office that most of these girls aren't prosecuted, where there's a suspicion they're "riding a beef" for someone else. Such lack of legal action is, of course, based on the ancient premise that it's better for 1,000 guilty persons to go free than for one innocent person to stand convicted.

Too many girls, however, have served prison terms, or are now serving prison terms, for offenses committed by their husbands, boyfriends, or pimps: They are martyrs, in most cases, to a love that never existed.

I have a tape recording that I play for individual girls whom I am seeking to help, for young women's church and civic groups and—on occasion—for the melancholy residents of homes for unwed mothers. The voice on the tape is pleasant. It is the voice of a 22-year-old man whose appearance is equally pleasant, and who recently "kicked" a $150-a-day drug habit. The recording is as follows:

> Man, I've messed around with a lot of girls. Every junkie has. I never had any feelings for them. Not one of them. Oh, I'd tell them I did. I'd put down a real good rib, but if I ever got pulled up, man, I'd more than likely give them a real good head-strumming. I don't recall ever having a girl I didn't beat.

Roses from a Dark Garden

I don't think I ever turned out a square girl, though. A junkie with a real strung-out habit, he don't have time for square girls, the time it takes to court 'em and turn 'em out; and my monkey weighed 40 pounds! Mostly, the girls that worked for me, their first old man had turned them out, or some junkie would get busted and I'd take over his girls, or I just got them off the streets, where they were hustlin' solo.

They were all dope fiends. Most of them, they had burning habits and no connections. They were having to pay high, sometimes double, to score. I had connections. My brother, sister, uncle—they're all pushers. Pushers, they don't like to do two things, if they can get around them: They don't like to move, sell, or deal, that is, at night, and they don't like to deal with people who run their heads, you know, talk too much.

A lot of girls run their heads. A doll blows her cool (doesn't use sound judgment, loses her temper), and she's done messed up a good thing.

A lot of the girls I had, they were real race horses. They could really turn them tricks. They'd turn the money over to me and I'd buy dope with it. They'd fix between tricks. A girl with a real strung-out habit, she'll get out and hustle them marks. She'll do anything to beat people for their money.

Sometimes, when the vice squad had the heat on, I'd put the girls to boosting, which is shoplifting, or we'd go bipping. Bipping is where you burglarize and rob a house in broad daylight, maybe even while someone is home.

Or maybe I'd put the girls in a house around the state. Not just any house, but one where the action is fast. A looker who's a race horse, she can make $200 or more a day, and keep $75.00 of every $100 she makes. Actually, I got the money. A madam mostly always

119

turns over a girl's earnings to her pimp, the guy who contracted her into the house.

The trouble with putting a girl in a spot—that's what a house is called, too—she can't stay too long. If a spot has a steady clientele, they like variety. A house is a good place to train a girl, though.

I seldom had sex relations with any of my girls. A broad, she's hooked, she don't do it for pleasure, and a junkie with an oil burner, all he can think of is dope. Sex ain't really exciting to a dope fiend. It's just a commodity he or she exports.

Junkies, they're coconuts. All dope addicts are crazy, in my book. They're animals in another world, a world you can't know or understand unless you've experienced it. . . .

In the more than 15 years since I quit being a hoodlum and became a minister to hoodlums, I have watched the traffic in prostitution and dope become one of the most vicious rackets in the nation.

I link the two evils because I can't separate them. On the bulletin board of my being is a black roll on which is listed the names of more than 50 men and women, former friends and associates from my street gang days or characters whom I attempted to lead to Christ and salvation. Each of them died a violent death : by gun, knife, club or "hot shot."

Houston police traced 13 of the homicides to a seething war for control of prostitution in Houston and the rest of Texas. I know from my own knowledge that all of the others had used dope or were using dope, and that all their lives had fringed or centered on prostitution at one time or another.

I remember L., a gamine with a lovely face, a lush figure and a lust for luxury. Her environment conditioned her to prostitution, and she entered the profession willingly for, what to her, was easy money. She had her luxuries, earned by her talents as a call girl: the minks, the jewels, the big cars, all that the glittering web displays to entice foolish girls from the lower levels of society. Hers was a fascinating and gay life, which is part of the delusion; but it was also frenetic, which is part of the cost. Somewhere along the line, she started using pills—barbiturates—to bolster her vitality and alleviate her fatigue; and she admitted that the "red birds" and "yellow jackets" also eased her conscience. Goof balls, like weed, are merely a preliminary to the use of heroin. L. was proof of the delights promised but never delivered—after addiction—by the white powder.

Within a year, she was working in a house, a common prostitute. Within two years, she was a dull-eyed, emaciated girl of the streets, selling her favors for any price that would go toward the $7.00 she needed for a capsule of heroin and an hour's cessation of the fury that ravaged her body day and night.

Then there came a day when police, called by the keeper of the cheap hotel where she was rooming, found her dead on her bed, her frail wrists slashed and her "trick book," with its list of prominent clients contained within, under her pillow. It was her only memento from the "good days" she had known. She was 24 years old.

I remember M., a girl from a prominent family, who was fascinated by hoodlums and dated them for kicks. She used heroin for kicks, too, until she was hooked—and a sizeable fortune, left by her parents, was squandered on dope. After that, M. had to get her heroin like every other junkie—through theft, prostitution, forgery, burglary and robbery. M. had a flair for publicity and was once quoted on the front pages of the newspapers—during the course of one of her numerous trials—as saying: "I want to marry Lucky Luciano and go live in Shanghai because Lucky has all the dope in the world, and Shanghai has all the sin!"

121

M. never achieved either ambition. She died in a Chicago flophouse of an overdose of heroin.

More recently, there was J. who led a quiet life, and a respectable one, until she met Chuck.

Chuck was ruggedly handsome, and suave; and to a department store clerk like J., who had been reared in a small, staid, rural community, he was a most exciting personality. He was gallant: He opened car doors for her, lit her cigarettes and stood when she left or returned to their table in a restaurant or bar. He sent her flowers, gave her expensive perfume and deluged her with other gifts. He was obviously a man of means; and when she inquired as to the means, Chuck told her he was in "investments." This was easy for her to believe.

It wasn't nearly so easy for her to enter into an affair with him for she had had strict moral upbringing, and illicit sex was repugnant to her. She salved her scruples, however, with Chuck's promises to marry her.

Then one night, in a distant city where she'd gone for a weekend of fun with Chuck, came the rude shock. Chuck was a procurer for a call girl ring, and J. was the ring's newest conscript. She learned that night, and in the several days and nights that followed, that Chuck was hardly a candidate for the All-American gentleman. When she refused to willingly become a prostitute, he spread-eagled her on the bed, tied her wrists and ankles to the corner-posts, gagged her with a handkerchief and beat her repeatedly with his belt, a length of rope and a wire clothes-hanger that had been straightened out. After several days, dazed, exhausted and in shock from pain, lack of food and fear, J. succumbed. That night she was placed in a house of prostitution for "care and training."

I learned J.'s story several years later, long after she had parted with Chuck. The short time I knew J., she was an embittered woman with a deep hatred and distrust for men—even preachers—but she wasn't a junkie. She had found another antidote for shame: alcohol. She drank herself to death; and though the inquest verdict wasn't suicide, I've always felt it should have been.

Thank God, the ending is not always so tragic.

There is R., a tiny brunette, with a terrible scar on her neck that high collars can't completely hide. The scar is a mark of R.'s victory over thyroid cancer, which she developed as a child. She fought the deadly killer for eight years, and one day the doctors declared her "miraculously" cured. But R.'s miracle was yet to come.

The years of using drugs to combat the pain of the cancer had made of R. a "medical addict," although she was unaware of the fact. Subconsciously, however, her body yearned for drugs. Here is her story, as she told it to me:

I guess I would have been a square the rest of my life, but I met and married Jim. I didn't know he was a character until after we'd been married several months, and then he got busted for a burglary. He beat the case, and I stayed with him because I loved him. I didn't know he was using dope until one day I saw him and 10 or 12 others having a blast with horse.

I learned then that he had a paper-a-day habit, which is a $50-habit, and he'd turned to stealing to supply his habit.

I tried to get him to stop using dope, but I guess I didn't try very hard. He talked me into using it instead.

I don't know why I started using horse. I knew what dope did to a person. It's just one of those things. You don't think about it, and then when you do, it's too late.

When I thought about it, I had a $50-a-day habit, too. Jim kept me down—on the stuff—until he was busted again for burglary. He went to the joint, and I went to hustling.

I'd been hustling before, of course. Jim turned me out. But I never wanted to hustle. And I didn't want to be a dope fiend!

She's not anymore. She "kicked" the habit the only way you can really kick it—through accepting Jesus Christ.

And there is A. Sometimes when I'm a guest pastor at a certain church, I stop in at one of the Sunday school classes to exchange a smile and a word with a willowy, handsome woman who teaches that class. A., like me, was a product of the street gangs. At 16, she was married to a weedhead, and at 17 she divorced him when he went to prison for assault to murder. She married again at 19. Her husband was a musician who was "half-hep." I can recall A.'s words, too, the night she and her husband came to me for help—two frightened children fleeing a demon they'd unleashed:

Pat was just messing around with dope. A lot of musicians do, you know. He wasn't a hoodlum. One night, however, another band member said to him, "Why don't you turn your old lady on?" and Pat asked me if I wanted to joy-pop.

I figured shooting horse was like drinking, so I said sure. Well, you know the story. We both were hooked. I had a job as a clerk in an oil company. I'd fix at work, and then I'd have to flash—throw up—and I kept nodding out at my desk. The girl next to me was puzzled, but I put some sort of story on her. I only worked a month after I got strung out, and then I started writing hot checks to supply me and Pat. He had sold his instruments and was stealing everything in sight.

I got busted, a federal rap. The judge sent me to

Lexington for the cure, but you know those kind of cures. I did six months and was released. I scored and fixed as soon as I got off the train.

Pat was still real strung out and miserable. We couldn't scrape up enough, just stealing, to supply us both. Pat would have turned me out to hustle—I'd have done it myself—but my brother told Pat, "If you turn out my sister, I'll kill you." It shook both of us. Pat asked me to call around town and see if there wasn't some place he and I could take the cure that wasn't a prison or a hospital. A boy named Bob told me about Teen Liberators. You know the rest. . . .

I do know the rest. It's wonderful. Pat, too, is cured of dope addiction—cured through his belief in the power and love of Jesus.

There are many others who can be saved in a similar manner, and there are a growing number of pastors who are aiding me in local programs to salvage the lives of lost young girls.

Not the least of these is a middle-aged minister who, until recently, had tended strictly to his own flock, blissfully unaware of the carnal and venal problems of the world until I spoke at his church one Sunday. He was genuinely shocked and concerned.

"Can you speak again this afternoon, Brother Gage? I want you to speak often, to teach us how we may help," he implored.

I shook my head. "I will speak again, but not this afternoon. I have been invited to speak at an assembly at a home for unwed mothers."

"Then may I go with you?" he asked.

I took him with me. His initiation into "missionary" work in the stone jungles of civilization is a pungent memory that still brings a wry smile to his lips.

125

## Pulpit in the Shadows

I don't really know how to categorize promiscuity, and the many resulting cases of pregnancy, among our unmarried young women. It is a problem that is only partially linked to the underworld, but it is a problem with which the Church must be concerned, also. The sympathy and concern of my companion was certainly aroused that afternoon, as we sat informally among the group of teen-age girls whose bellies reflected their indiscretions and whose faces reflected a variety of emotions—shame, indifference, hope, bitterness.

The pastor was especially moved by the plight of one girl, an 18-year-old whose condition was a result of her clandestine affair with one of her high school teachers; and as he talked to her, the pastor reached over and patted her on the arm in a fatherly fashion.

The father image, however, had suffered somewhat with this particular girl. She knocked the pastor's hand away.

"Watch it, Reverend!" she snapped brusquely. "That's what put me in here!"

# 8
# "Hey, Man—Come Preach My Funeral!"

"I HAVE EATEN YOUR BREAD AND SALT,
I HAVE DRUNK YOUR WATER AND WINE,
THE DEATHS YE DIED I HAVE WATCHED BESIDE,
AND THE LIVES THAT YE LED WERE MINE."
———RUDYARD KIPLING

I stood in the pulpit and looked down at Robby in his coffin. His features were natural, almost smiling; and as I looked upon his dead face, Robby's voice—lightly mocking, vibrant, tinged with defiance—echoed down the corridor of my thoughts:

"Hey, man—when I get it, I want you to preach my funeral!"

Beneath the crisp white shirt and the dark blue coat that were his grave clothes, Robby had four bullet holes in his chest.

I lifted my eyes to the men and women who sat with decorum in the pews of the small chapel. Almost without exception they were thieves, prostitutes, dope addicts, burglars, bippers and hustlers. It looked like a police lineup.

As I regarded them over the body of the man they mourned, I breathed a short prayer: "Oh, Lord God, let me bring some of these people to You today. Let me move just one of them to Your glory, Lord. I have walked with all of them in wickedness. Let me walk with one of them in Jesus!"

Then came the question that always plagued me on these occasions. Which one of them would next die by the gun or the knife? For which one would I next preach, while my soul cried out in protest? How many had to die before one of them would see?

I began to speak, lapsing into the argot of the hoodlum: "I knew Robby. We were junior jivers together. He was my friend. His friends were my friends. We blasted pot together. We scored together. We were busted together. Then I found Christ, and was born again. . . ."

I turned the funeral into a revival service. I stopped each one afterwards, as they filed past the casket to have their last look at Robby. I begged each to turn to Christ, and some said they would; but I knew from their tone of voice that they wouldn't. And one, like Robby, grinned impudently, slapped my arm and said, "Reverend, you sure can preach. I want you to preach my funeral when I get wiped out!"

The words rang in my ears all the way home; and "The Plan" surged back into my thoughts—stronger and more urgent. It was a giant fiery pinwheel in my mind, spinning and clicking off names and numbers: thousands of young people under 21 called to the attention of officials each year in just this city alone . . . Donnie dead of a hot shot . . . thousands of illegitimate births in Houston annually . . . Kip shot dead . . . 19 percent of the murders in America are committed by persons under 21 . . . Jamie stabbed to death in a brawl . . . thousands of teen-agers arrested in Houston in one year . . . Shirley a suicide, Beth dead from an overdose of heroin . . . delinquent kids, thousands of them, troubled, confused, and homeless . . . Tab with his belly torn out by a shotgun blast . . . a murder every eight hours, a burglary every eight minutes . . . juvenile crime up 100 per cent in the past 10 years.

And then the cruel fact: In Texas, there was no Christian place for juvenile delinquents, problem young people and teen-age addicts except reform schools, prisons and federal narcotics hospitals.

I decided that I'd build one. God and I would. Jesus Christ would be architect and the cornerstone.

Such a Christian center had been a goal of mine for years. It was a dream born in my heart with Donnie's death, and never once over the years had I ever doubted that it was a dream sanctioned by God. He had planted the seed. He would make it a success.

Donnie's death—a spear wound in my spirit.

Donnie came from a solid, respectable family. He was the only boy, an amiable, clean-cut kid who loved sports, kept a horse and had every right to look forward to a fine future. Then, when he was 12, his father died. Of course, Donnie still had a mother and sister who loved him; and he had his horse, which he loved. He might have had a future had he not been entrapped by a street gang—mine.

When he was 13, I "turned him on"—taught him to blast weed. Having put him on "pot," I left him to go his own way. Once introduced to dope, you can't go but one way—down. Donnie was soon hooked on heroin, and, like all junkies, stealing and robbing to feed his habit.

If I turned Donnie on, I also attempted to turn him off. Shortly after I was ordained into the ministry, Donnie appeared at a revival that I was conducting. Like other former hoodlum associates, he was curious to see if I was "putting down a hype" with "this religious kick." I convinced him that I wasn't shamming, and he began to appear regularly at churches where I conducted services. Donnie would "fix" on horse and then come hear me preach on the evils of dope. One night he brought 15 other hoodlums with him. They were all "boxed out" on horse, really high. They all pleaded tearfully that they wanted to get off the stuff.

Donnie accepted Christ during one of my youth revivals. My heart was lightened with joy, and a bit of the burden on my soul was lessened.

When next I heard of Donnie, he was in the hospital. He had been shot and wounded during an attempted robbery!

131

I was in a distant city and could not go to him personally, so I wrote him a letter. It was a missive full of spelling errors and grammatical boo-boos, for I was still unschooled; and it was full of anger—directed both at Donnie and myself—for he had been my first major convert, and I felt a sense of personal failure. Could no part of the guilt that streaked my soul ever be erased?

Here is the letter:

Dear Donnie,

Well how is the big timer making it. P. sent me your picture out of the paper! The Lord told me to take time out and write you! I just wonder when you bunch of punks or going to get right with yourself and God! I get in mail letters from everywhere and everybody. The other day in the mail I received a letter frome P. L. He was before your time! He was a tuff guy. He was a chacter one of the biggest dope heads I ever knew! I seen him cut a fellow ear to ear one night. He is now in the pentintery! He read about me in the paper and said he was glad to know I changed my life. He said it was too late for him to change he was in prison all of his friends was gone except his mother & dad! He is in a bad fix! I wish I had the leter I would send it to you! I get leters all the time from my old 'cats' in the Pen! They don't like it! Their lives are wasted for the devil! I remember that night you came to hear me preach you made a decision for <u>Christ</u>. <u>You lied to God and he is going to come out winner!</u> You cant win <u>against</u> God. <u>The Bible says</u>, 'What so ever a man sows that what he will also <u>reap</u>! You are reaping <u>bad</u>! Yes you think it is smart and big now but you wont in the end! I never will forget the first time I got my picture in the paper for being a tough guy. I thought I was something! But even today I am still reaping what I sowed! I give you six months unless you change you will be in the <u>Pen</u>! You are 17 years old now just <u>ripe</u> all of my bunch everyone of them is in the <u>joint</u>! I am not talking about the sprouts like you and P. you are headed soon. Dope has got a holt of your lives! I praise God that he saved me and got me off the stuff. The reason I am writing you is because I belive it is part my fault. Do you know who brought the first stick of weed to 'Podunk' Freddie Gage. All of the bunch out their dudn't know what it was. I turned the hold bunch out! I wold give my right arm if that was not on my mine. I get leters from my old buddies in the Pen. T. N. was a good guy till he met me! B. C.! A charcter live cant win. L. I. shot to death. S. stabbed to death. J. S. turnkey killed him most of these guys are way before you time. Donnie something happen to you that night you made that decsion for Christ didnt it. But you cood not take the razing from the boys! I did now I am on top married have a son. I am in college they are in prison who is on top. You had better think about these things. Paul C. I am proud of him he is on the right road! I guess you have made fun but he will win you will lose! I will be in a revival in Gatesville reform school the last week of this month hundreds of boys on the same road you are headed for Hell. You are young Donnie you have a life in front of you! I would like to see you get right with God. Leave town start to school or college or some-where else. Start to a Christian College. Be something in life for God! Check over your life take inventory. What you are today in the eyes of the world a 'punk' a 'hoodlum' a 'dope head.' Just stop 5 minutes when you get this letter and think. In the eyes of God you are a sinner. Hell is a terrible place. May God help you get on the right road! Pray for yourself and I will pray for you.

> Your buddy when the rest or gone
> Evan. Freddie Gage
> 'God Way is the Right Way'

I was wrong about Donnie going to prison within six months. Within six months he was dead. The "occupational hazard" of the junkie, an overdose of narcotics, claimed him. His was the first funeral sermon I preached. His mother came to me following the funeral and gave me back the letter I had written Donnie.

"There are a lot of youngsters like Donnie, boys who have gone wrong," she cried. "Why can't something be done to help them before it's too late? Why? Why?"

In the years that followed, I read and reread the letter I had written in vain; and each time, his mother's plaintive plea resounded in my ears. "And why couldn't something be done?" I asked myself. I asked hundreds of pastors, too. They were sympathetic. Many wanted to help, but the project entailed too vast a sum of money for any one church to support, and most congregations took a dim view of the plan. I learned that a lot of church people were more interested in the church organ, the church's stained glass windows and church artifacts than they were in lost souls. They had made of their churches only expensive caskets in which they had placed the body, not the spirit, of our Lord.

I did not get discouraged. The Lord bolstered my spirit each time I was rebuffed; and my determination to found a Christian center designed to reach and rehabilitate troubled youngsters grew each time I had to stand over the body of a former friend and sermonize on his wasted life.

More than a dozen of those I preached to their graves were victims of a long and bloody war among the city and state vice barons for control of the flesh market. The police referred to the series of consociate killings as "the battle of the pimps" and one newspaperman, after several gangland-style shootouts, wrote that "Houston's panderers are playing a game of ring-around-the pistol."

Robby was a casualty. In a way, he initiated the succession of slayings. A call girl was strangled to death, and her pimp was arrested and charged with the slaying. Before he could be brought to trial, however, Robby shot him to death in a quarrel he himself provoked. A tender-hearted jury listened to his plea of self-defense, and meted out only a five-year prison term. Robby appealed even that light sentence, but the appeal was never heard by a higher court. While out on bond, Robby continued his activities as a peddler of female flesh but made the mistake of raiding the "harem" of a prince of panderers known as the "Bedroom Bedouin." The dark-eyed descent of desert warriors encountered Robby at a bawd's ball one night and emptied a pistol in Robby's direction. The "Bedouin" was acquitted—on the premise that Robby was armed and had threatened him—but the verdict was set aside by another pimp. He invited the "Bedouin" to a party and shot him through the head. The killer drew 30 years.

Tab was also a victim of the carnal war, although officially his death was attributed to a disagreement over cards.

Tab, as a sprout, had been one of my subordinates in the Black Shirts. He was a creature of the slums, a pimp from the moment he became aware of man's predilection for woman—an awareness that came at a very early age—and a pillhead. Like many pimps, he married a "hep square." She wouldn't hustle dates, she wouldn't steal and she wouldn't mess with dope; but she had no overt objection to Tab's preoccupation with all three.

She called me one morning. "Have you heard about Tab?"

"No, I haven't," I said, sensing what would come next.

"He's been killed. He wanted you to preach his sermon, he always said. He said you'd do it up real fine."

As a funeral, it was almost a fiasco. When I arrived at the funeral home and stepped from my car, I noticed a stream of characters exiting hurriedly from the rear door.

I grabbed one by the arm. "What's the score, man? Where's everybody splitting to?"

He grimaced. "Anywhere. The Man's out front and no one can fade (endure) the heat."

I managed to halt the exodus, explaining that I'd go out front and talk to the police—it turned out that they were members of the vice squad. They were sitting in their car, observing everyone entering the funeral home chapel. Those entering had been reduced to a trickle. Tab's friends, approaching the funeral home, would spot the pair of cops and drive on past without slowing down.

They appraised me coolly as I stepped to the squad car and leaned down to speak to the driver. The officer spoke first. "So you're the underworld preacher." It was a statement of fact, not a question; and the tone was neutral, which argued a measure of tolerance on the detective's part. I nodded.

"That's me, all right. And I'm here to ask you to leave. Not one of these hoods is going to be around for the preaching if you don't. They're all splitting in all directions!"

The other chuckled harshly. "So what? I don't imagine any of them dig sermons, anyway."

"Maybe not," I conceded. "But it may be the only time some of them will hear the word of God. It may be the only time I have a chance to persuade one of them to make a decision for Christ. Please, boys!"

The officers looked at one another and then both nodded. "You're right, Parson," said the driver. "You got your chance. Good luck." He started the engine, nodded again, and drove away.

An hour later, when I began to speak, the chapel was packed. Tab's was one of the largest gangland funerals I ever conducted. I drove his widow home from the cemetery; and, as if she could read my thoughts, she turned to me and said, "Something needs to be done to reach them, Freddie. I think you'll find that way."

I was determined to find that way—the only way, I felt—but all of the avenues which I explored for the ways and means to found a Christian center led to a dead end. I found enthusiasm aplenty—not a little among the underworld—but those financially able to underwrite the project were reluctant, for one reason or another, to do so. I cannot censure them.

Meanwhile, those who might have been helped by the institute that I envisioned continued to die their violent deaths. They peopled my dreams, and more than once I awakened with my ears full of mocking laughter and the reverberation of "Hey, man—come preach my funeral!"

I kept preaching their funerals, too. There was J.T.'s—he died of an overdose of heroin. There was Wally's funeral—he was "wiped out" for being a stoolie. And Squatty's—he died in the wreckage of a car he thought he could drive while all pilled up. And Shirley's—she overfixed. And Dolly's—she was given a "hot shot."

On one occasion, a young minister whom I had persuaded to accompany me to the funeral of a notorious figure listened and then grasped my arm as I sat down.

"Brother Gage, that wasn't much of a funeral message—but it was a tremendous evangelical sermon!" he said.

As a matter of fact, I spent little time on eulogies for those for whom I performed the last rites. Instead, I exhorted the mourners to give up their sinful ways. I ranted at them to accept Christ, to be born again, to become useful Christians and useful citizens before it was too late—as it was too late for him who lay in the coffin. I preached Hell's fire and damnation sermons.

Once, at the conclusion of a particularly impassioned lecture, I turned to find the organist regarding me with a rapt expression. She stopped me as I left the chapel. "Reverend Gage," she said, "I've been playing music at funerals for over 20 years, and you're the first preacher I've ever known who stepped up to that pulpit and told the people out front what they needed to hear!"

Although some of my fellow ministers regarded my fu-

neral preachments as unorthodox—"better suited to a revival meeting," one told me—I persuaded many hoodlums to
make a decision for Christ while standing at the casket of
one of their friends. When it was brought to my attention
that a large percentage of these converts later reverted to
their old ways and habits (dope habits, usually), I argued
that such regressions only accentuated the need for a Christian rehabilitation center.

On one occasion, preaching on the need for more missionary work among the criminal element, I was interrupted by
a pair of uniformed police officers, one of whom informed
the congregation that several youngsters had been caught in
the act of stripping cars on the church parking lot.

I abandoned my sermon. "This incident serves better
than words to illustrate the problem I came here to speak of,"
I told the fellowship. "Here you sit, secure and self-right-
eous in your beautiful church—and the police are out on
your parking lot picking up the very boys you need to
reach!"

One of my staunchest supporters in those days was a
grizzled old man with broad, square-fingered hands and
features perpetually set in sadness. His name was Walter,
and at one time he had been a guard on one of the state's
penal farms. Walter was a "high rider," a guard who sits
horseback a short distance from a field squad, which is
usually composed of 10 convicts. A "high rider" is charged
with stopping any convict who breaks from his squad or who
attacks the guard "carrying" (supervising on foot) the
squad. Generally, such convicts are stopped with a well-
placed .30–.30 slug.

One day another "high rider" stopped by Walter and
pointed out a dark-haired convict chopping cotton. "Watch
that'n, Walter. He's one of the sorriest sons any mother ever
whelped."

"Hey, Man—Come Preach My Funeral!"

Walter nodded. "I know," he replied softly. "He's my son!"

It was a statement of fact. Walter was the sire of what is still one of the most nefarious families in the Southwest, an outlaw clan whose children are weaned on wickedness.

Walter fathered three sons and three daughters. All of them went bad. Each one became a dope addict. Each one went to prison at least once. Each one chose an outlaw for a mate when he or she married, and each one of them married at least once. Each of them had children, and now some of the children are serving prison terms or are junkies themselves.

Walter was not a criminal himself, as the law defines a criminal. He was a drunkard. "I have to take the blame for their turning bad," he told me frankly. "I tolerated their childish misdeeds. I condoned their adult crimes. I made excuses for myself and them. All they had to do to get around me was to hand me a bottle of whiskey. Whiskey's as bad as dope, son, to some folks."

I recall driving to Walter's home on a summer day and noting a tent revival, conducted by a missionary society, in a field nearby. On impulse, I stopped and introduced myself to the evangelist heading the crusade. He was a stern-faced, dignified man. I nodded toward Walter's sprawling home, a short distance away.

"Have you made a visit there yet, Brother?" I asked.

The preacher's eyes widened. "Oh, no! They're gangsters!"

I nodded. "That's right. But Jesus Christ saved from the uppermost to the guttermost, and I've yet to meet a preacher better than Him. I was on my way to visit those people. Won't you join me?"

The evangelist nodded. "You're right, Brother Gage. Yes, I'll go with you."

## Pulpit in the Shadows

We walked to Walter's home, From the look of near-horror on his face, I doubted that the missionary had ever before encountered such squalor and wretchedness as he witnessed that day. A dozen or more of Walter's grandchildren played in the junk-cluttered yard. Some were naked, all were dirty and several of the tots displayed tatoos on various parts of their bodies!

A six-year-old regarded us with a practiced eye and decided we weren't the "fuzz."

"Did you come to score?" he asked candidly.

Walter was not at home. Several teen-agers and adults were inside the house, which was filthy and permeated with foul odors. All those inside recognized me. I recognized the situation. The missionary and I had arrived during a dope party. Everyone in the house was "high," and four or five were "on the nod." The pastor and I made an effort to talk to them, but it was useless; so we left some religious tracts and took our leave.

The missionary shuddered. "My God—I did not dream such things existed!"

I had grown up with Walter's children. We had joy-popped horse and blasted weed together. The boys had been members of my gang. They were my first "targets" when I ventured among the underworld as a minister seeking souls to lead to Christ.

None of the boys or girls made a decision for the Lord, but Walter did. He stayed with his decision, too, and over the years became my partner in attempting to lead his children and grandchildren to salvation.

Walter attended several funerals at which I officiated. One was that of a son-in-law, who died in an alcoholic stupor. Another was one of his own sons, who overfixed on drugs.

There was one other funeral at which I officiated that Walter attended, too. His own. One night, I was called to his bedside in the hospital where he had been taken following a heart attack. I could see that Walter was near death as he reached for my hand.

"I held out till you got here, Freddie," he said with a weary smile. "I had to ask you to keep after them—don't ever give up on them." Walter was dead before I could reply.

I remember the day my intention to found a Christian youth center crystalized. It was when I preached Sonny's funeral. I knew that day that I would soon give up the evangelical circuit to work toward the establishment of the center.

And one day, driving with a friend through the downtown area of Houston, I saw the "whole way" house I envisioned. It was a huge, three-story relic of the city's turn-of-the-century splendor, sitting sedately among massive oaks. A "For Sale" sign was displayed in the yard.

"That's it!" I exclaimed. "That's my center!"

"Freddie, that house and that land, this close in, would cost a fortune! Where will you get the money?"

"I'll get it. The Lord will provide it."

# 9
# A House
# "Within a Yard of Hell!"

"PREPARE THY WORK WITHOUT, AND
MAKE IT FIT FOR THYSELF IN THE FIELD;
AND AFTERWARDS BUILD THINE HOUSE."
—PROVERBS 24:27

I could not pass the old house by. I had to get out and inspect it. There was an old man—the caretaker—puttering about the parklike grounds. He was as gnarly and cross-grained as the great oaks dotting the vast lawn, but he regarded me alertly from beneath brows sculptured by 80 or more years.

"Do you know how much the realtor wants for this house?" I asked, pointing to the FOR SALE sign.

The old man's answer was brief and laced with vinegary amusement. "Yep. The heirs want $225,000 for it."

I was not surprised. Through the trees, hulking above the surrounding neighborhood, was the lattice-work skyline of Houston, "Bagdad-on-the-Bayou," where property on Main Street was sold casually for $2,000 per front inch! It would not be too many years before the mushrooming "downtown" area engulfed this once regal district.

"What are you going to do with this house, if you buy it?" the old man asked. There was no spleen in the question, but the tone of the old man's voice clearly indicated that he didn't regard me as a buyer.

"I want to turn it into a Christian center for young boys," I replied, smiling. "I want to reach delinquent boys—teen-

145

age gangs, dope addicts, kids in trouble and kids with no homes. I want to give them a new start in life through Christ. Don't you think that's worthwhile?"

A sudden warmth flooded the old man's face. "I sure do, Mister, and it'd make a good place for what you got in mind. Care to look it over?"

I will never forget the feeling I had as I followed him up the wide stone steps, across the tiled veranda and through the tall double doors that served as a front entrance. It was a feeling of reverence, of fulfillment, of promise; and I seemed to sense the presence of Someone else, Someone who had said, two thousand years past, "In my Father's house are many mansions . . ."

The old man flicked a switch and chandeliers high above us illuminated the large entrance hall. The plaster on the walls was dirty and peeling, the woodwork was grimy and dusty, the carpets on the floor were worn and faded and a musty odor permeated the air; but there was a dignity and grandeur still clinging to the old house—a haughtiness that awed me.

Space! Space! Space! The roominess of the great home set my soul to singing. On either side of the entrance were sitting rooms, both of which contained a fireplace. The one on the south side contained some heavy, hand-carved furniture and opened onto a large sun porch that was enclosed by high French windows. This first floor also contained a spacious dining room, a living room, a great kitchen and a capacious breakfast room.

A broad, handcarved stairway led to the second floor. Halfway up, an expansive alcove had been built, and it contained cushioned benches beneath stained glass windows—as beautiful as any I had ever seen. Surely, many a passage from the Bible had been read here in this quiet nook, lighted by the sun streaming through the lovely windows.

146

## A House "Within a Yard of Hell!"

I followed the old man on up to the second floor. This floor was equally impressive: three bedrooms, a sitting room and a breakfast nook, all opening onto a wide balcony that extended around three sides of the house.

The third floor was a thrill in itself. It was one huge—50 feet by 30 feet—play room, ideal for a dormitory! In addition to all I have detailed, there were also three and one-half bathrooms and storage closets and clothes closets galore, some big enough to be converted into bedrooms!

I went back downstairs and outside, convinced that the Lord had steered me to the old mansion.

"It's perfect for what I have in mind," I remarked. "It's a big home."

The old man nodded. "Yep. Eleven thousand square feet of living space, not counting the double garage and servant's quarters in the rear. That's where I live."

The old man regarded me wonderingly. "You got the money to buy this house, boy?"

I laughed. "No, but my Father has."

"Your dad own a business of some kind?"

"My Father owns all the cattle upon a thousand hills," I replied. I walked away, toward my car, leaving the old man with a speculative look on his crinkled features.

That night, I called several board members of the Freddie Gage Evangelistic Association, Inc., and told them of my find. The board president expressed the opinion of all those I contacted. "Freddie, you know we will do whatever we can to help you—we are certainly in favor of your project. But $225,000! We simply don't have it. We're barely able—on the contributions we're receiving—to meet the expenses for your various revival commitments, not to mention other necessary disbursements."

"I know that," I replied. "I just wanted the board to know about the house. I am depending on God to provide the means to acquire it."

Someone once said that the success of any great moral enterprise does not depend on numbers. Nevertheless, I called several ministers and persuaded them to accompany me in a group to the realtor's office the following day. Each of them was concerned with my ministry among Houston's hoodlums, and each was desirous of seeing a Christian center such as I propounded become a reality.

The realtor was one of Houston's more successful in the field, with offices in a glistening new downtown skyscraper. The realtor, himself, in dress and deportment, reflected the opulence that surrounded him; but he welcomed us cordially, and I sensed that behind the brisk business mien was a gentle and sensitive nature. He listened without interruption while I explained what I wanted to do with the old house.

Then he said, "Mr. Gage, the heirs are asking a $20,000 down payment on a long-term note, which I feel is very reasonable. Can you pay down that amount? Or, perhaps I should say, how much can you pay down?"

"Nothing," I admitted. "But I can raise all of the money eventually."

The realtor regarded me with a quizzical smile. "I'm intrigued by your passion for this project. Do you really think it will work?"

"I do," I replied frankly. "I believe addiction to any drug or narcotic can be broken through the power of Jesus Christ. I believe all things are possible through Jesus Christ."

I took a deep breath. "I believe God sent me here!"

The realtor regarded me steadily for what seemed like an hour, and then he smiled and nodded. "All right, Mr. Gage, I'll write the letter to the heirs, outlining your goals and detailing your financial situation. There are three of them, and any disposition of the property must be unanimously agreed upon."

The next several weeks passed as sluggishly as years. I

had no wish to pester the realtor—I certainly didn't want to irritate him—but I could not resist calling him at intervals. Each time, the answer was the same: He had not heard from the heirs.

I did not lose faith, however, that God would make the old home available to me for His work.

The day finally arrived when the realtor left a message with my answering service (I was out of town, conducting a revival) for me to drop by his office at my earliest convenience. My earliest convenience, of course, was immediately after the message was relayed to me. My throat was dry, and my heart was pounding as his secretary ushered me into his private office.

The realtor sensed the suspense that gripped me and dispensed with the formalities and small talk. "Reverend Gage," he said, smiling, "The owners are delighted with the use to which you wish to put the house, and as a gesture of their support of your project, have authorized me to make the following offer:

"You may have the house for $165,000—$20,000 down and the remainder in equal monthly payments over a 20-year period, at a suitable interest rate, of course;

"Or, you may purchase the property for $150,000 cash;

"Or (and the smile on his face broadened), you may lease the home—month to month—for $250 per month, with option to buy!"

I was so elated that I felt like shouting for joy. My emotions at the moment were not unlike those of a proud father just informed of the birth of his first son. Perhaps such emotions were appropriate, for at that moment, Teen Liberators was born!

Purchasing the house for cash was out of the question. So (for the moment, at least) was any thought of buying the house over a 20-year period. The $20,000 down payment was a barrier I couldn't surmount. But I knew that I could meet the $250 a month rental—even if it meant paying it out of my salary and moving Barbara and the boys into the old mansion to live.

The board ruled that this wouldn't be necessary.

"We'll find the rent money easily enough, Freddie," some members of the board commented. "It's getting the funds to meet the other expenses of operating such a center that worries us!"

"We'll trust God to provide those expenses. He'll help us, you'll see," I assured them.

I contacted a lawyer, who agreed to handle the legal details of leasing the house and the chartering with the state (as required by law) of the center, and then sat down and began drawing up a master plan for the Lord's house of redemption.

I listed the services that the center would offer: spiritual and vocational therapy, school and college guidance and placement, family follow-up and counseling, a worker's training program, medical treatment for illnesses other than dope addiction, job placement and a restitutional program.

As Teen Liberators evolved on paper, I was staggered at the scope and the cost of the project—which I was launching on faith! The annual cost of the venture would approach $75,000!

"That's a minimum cost estimate, for 30 boys in residence, a staff of nine and part-time help," the auditor who prepared the figures told me. "But the estimate covers the full range—salaries, travel and transportation, building lease, utilities, telephone, building supplies and maintenance, food, clothing, laundry and cleaning, school fees and allowances, office supplies and equipment, accounting and legal fees, spiritual outreach and miscellaneous supplies and expenses."

The auditor scanned his work. "Of course, that doesn't

include the initial refurbishing and furnishing of the building," he added.

I shook off the shock induced by such astronomical (to me, anyway) sums and plunged ahead blithely. After all, Jesus Christ was the executive treasurer of the project, wasn't He? He'd find a way.

The next several weeks I spent canceling revivals which I had scheduled for the coming months, getting out a newsletter to supporters of the Freddie Gage Evangelistic Association—telling of our plans for the new center and its need—and extolling the merits of the Teen Liberators program to newspaper editors and Houston-area church groups. I spoke to youth groups, ministerial groups, missionary groups and even civic clubs.

"Fifty years ago, in the heart of Africa, a great modern missionary society sprung up," I told many of the groups. "Its founder, the Reverend C. T. Studd, had battled for God in China, then did a seven-year hitch for Christ in India. Finally, told by his superiors that he was too old to be useful any longer, he journeyed to Africa to found his own missionary society, a society that has since trained and sent more than 1,000 missionaries into the wilds of Africa, Asia and South and Central America—and into the stone jungles of the big cities. C. T. Studd's creed was expressed in the opening stanza of a poem he wrote:

> Some want to live within the sound
> Of church or chapel bell;
> I want to run a rescue shop
> Within a yard of hell.

"That's what Teen Liberators intends to do—run a rescue shop within a yard of hell!"

The response to my appeals was overwhelming—a measure of the goodness of man and the glory of God. On the day I had selected as the date to begin renovating the old mansion—which we had rented "as is"—teen-age boys and girls from churches throughout Houston appeared, lugging brooms, mops, pails, soap, wax, scrubbers, dust cloths, paint and paint brushes!

The dirt, dust and grime disappeared. Windows sparkled. Copper and brasswork shimmered brightly. The chandeliers and other light fixtures glittered. The woodwork, trim, wall paneling and stairway—through repeated applications of oil, wax and elbow grease—began to glow richly.

Adults came and went in a steady stream. One group brought a refrigerator. Another man brought a stove. Another had a crew unload a deep freeze! Carpenters swarmed over the house, repairing defects in the woodwork, and plumbers appeared to check and repair sinks, bathtubs, showers and commodes. Telephone men came and installed phones in the foyer and in the first and second floor chambers which had been designated as offices.

An aged man, who said he was a retired minister, came and began building an altar in the sitting room that I had selected as a chapel. Women appeared and began putting up curtains and setting up the kitchen.

The old house resembled an ant colony with all the activity—workers were toiling on every level and in every chamber!

Among those who appeared for "Operation Cleanup" was Jerry Bernard, a young minister who had made a decision for Christ at one of my campus revivals at Baylor. Jerry was an accomplished accordionist and a gifted singer, and had long been interested in my work.

"Jerry, I'd like you to be the associate director in residence," I said. "Will you take the job?"

Jerry didn't hesitate. "I can move in tonight, if you'd like."

## A House "Within a Yard of Hell!"

"No," I laughed. "I don't think anyone will be staying here tonight."

As a matter of fact, however, several people did spend the night, including our first "hoodlum-in-residence." I had anticipated that it would be several days before the building would be ready for occupancy so that Teen Liberators could begin operations. The Lord, however, had different plans.

Who else knew of little Pablo, son of an indigent family, and his need for shoes? In the midst of the swirl of cleaning activity, the boy's face, wistful and dejected, edged into my mind; and I could not put his image away. Finally, I laid down my scrub brush and drove downtown to a shoe store, although there was no urgency about the matter—it was August in Texas, barefoot weather for children.

I was still questioning my own sudden actions as I walked from the store to my car, the shoes in a box under my arm.

"Hey, Rev! Don't you speak to anyone but squares these days?" The voice was raucous but friendly.

I turned to see Bat and Pinky, two North Side hoods, approaching. They were swaggering arrogantly, but I sensed the fear and necessity that whittled at their veneer of insolence. And suddenly I knew why I had been sent on a shoe-buying errand today, and by whom.

I smiled at Bat and Pinky. "Man, if ever I saw two junkies out hustlin' to score, you two are it."

"Aw, Rev, don't put us down like that!" Pinky protested. "We ain't hooked. Maybe a joy-pop now and then, huh, Bat?" Bat nodded. He sniffed nervously. His eyes were beginning to water.

"Don't try to rib me," I rasped. "Look at Bat. Look at yourself! It's about time somebody told you the truth about your habit! You've been lying, cheating, stealing, and working angles ever since you got hooked, both of you! You thought you were different, didn't you? You thought you'd never get hooked. You thought you'd never have to mug or break in to feed your habit. Smart, aren't you? You never thought you'd end up like a beggar—living from one fix to the other. You still can't admit you're hooked.

"Well, quit fooling yourselves! You're junkies! You're hooked! You're losing your life and your soul, both of you! You're not going to control your habits—it's going to control you. But there is a cure—a permanent cure!"

I told them about Teen Liberators and our mission.

"I'd like both of you to go back with me," I said. "But if you like the kind of life you're living, don't—but pass the word on the grapevine, will you? Tell the people you talk to not to come out there working an angle. I just want hypes who are sick of dope and fed up with the needle, and who want to start a new life!"

Bat and Pinky shifted nervously, anxious to be about their search for a connection. I knew the signs. I knew the weight of the monkey that rode each of their backs. I knew neither of them would go with me right then.

Pinky showed up at the center that night!

"Okay, Cat," he sighed. "Let's try your Jesus cure!"

He hadn't scored for any H. A codeine-laced cough syrup had carried him through the afternoon and had given him the courage to come to the center. He looked around and then walked to the stairs and slumped on the bottom step. We had no chairs.

Several of the young volunteers—who had continued their labors after darkness fell—gawked at Pinky. For many, it was their first look at a real live junkie. I'm sure one or two of them expected him to sprout horns and a tail momentarily. Pinky paid them no heed as he lifted his eyes to me.

"You're right, Cat," he said dolefully. "I've got a real oil burning habit. And right now I'm in bad shape!"

There was not a bunk or a bed in the house, but I didn't intend that Pinky should leave and come back later. Teen

Liberators began operating on the instant. I sent several kids scurrying about, and they returned with a cot, an air mattress, bed linens, blankets, towels, soap and other items that I knew we'd need. By the time we got the cot ready in an upstairs bedroom (one with a bathroom), Pinky's nose was running, his eyes were watering and he was beginning to yawn frequently—the classic signs of an addict in the first stages of withdrawal. Only Pinky and I knew the hell that was in store for him over the next 72 hours.

There are few tortures known to man as excruciating, both mentally and physically, as that an addict experiences while kicking his habit "cold turkey." I selected three of the stronger, more mature boys from among the volunteers and sent the others home. I warned the three that stayed that none of them would get any rest that night and probably none the next day. All three vowed to go without rest as long as necessary.

The four of us sat on the edge of Pinky's cot—two on each side—and talked to him. At intervals, we prayed or read from the Bible, but as the hours wore on, Pinky complained that we were "running" our heads too much. Some addicts prefer a minimum of conversation during withdrawal.

Around midnight, Pinky's ordeal began in earnest. He complained that his muscles hurt; and he began to twitch, to kick and to sweat. He groaned and writhed against the pain. He played his glittering eyes over the faces of the three young church workers.

"Do you kids know what I'd do for a fix right now?" he gasped. "I'd steal from my mother. I'd kill to get a fix." His taut body arched in pain.

I massaged his aching body with the electric hand massager that had long been a part of my first-aid kit for junkies; but still the pain worsened as his nerves shrieked out for the dope now denied his system. Pinky was convulsed with cramps. He vomited, and even when his stomach was emptied of all fluids, he continued to be racked by spasms of retching.

He shook from chills. He burned with fever. Diarrhea added to the indignities inflicted on his physical being, and Pinky clutched his face and cried out against the headache that pounded at his brain. Goose bumps covered his body. He was so ill he refused all offers of food and drink.

We gave him hot and cold baths. We bathed his face with cold cloths, and we packed him in hot towels when the anguish of muscle spasms again gripped him. A hot water bottle was placed beneath the back of his neck to ease the stiffness of his spinal column.

Pinky was still in intense pain when the young volunteers returned to resume their cleaning tasks the next day—a repeat of the previous day. Adult church workers and ministers trooped in and out of the center in droves, bringing food, items of furniture, gifts and donations of money with which to buy other household necessities and supplies. God was providing, as I had had faith He would, and my spirit shouted hosannas. My weariness fled in the light of His love so amply demonstrated.

Many of those who came that day visited Pinky in his private torture chamber. I cautioned them against talking to him or asking him needless questions, but many visited the sickroom without my knowledge. Had I been able to instruct them, I know that they would have heeded me, for they were all good men, Christian men. Their interest in Pinky was wholly understandable. After all, he—and others of his ilk—was the basis of this center.

On the afternoon of his second day at the center, Pinky fell into a fitful sleep, and I felt that I could leave the center for a few hours. I went on a tour of Army surplus stores, seeking bargains in beds and bunks. The congregations of several churches had pledged payment for the sleeping needs of the center. I found a dozen suitable bunks at one store and received a discount when the owner learned how the beds would be used—I returned to the center exultantly.

The volunteers were still going about their chores industriously, but a definite gloom pervaded the atmosphere. Then I saw, sprawled on the stairway, the three boys who had been keeping vigil beside Pinky. Their faces were weary and dejected.

"What are you doing down here? Why aren't you upstairs?" I demanded.

"He's gone," one of them replied dully. "He said all these people bugged him, that he didn't like all these people running their heads, and he said he was splitting, whatever that means. I guess he meant he was leaving."

"Gone!" Stunned, I sank down in a chair near the door. Pinky was gone! We had lost the first "patient" to be admitted to our "spiritual hospital." A sense of defeat began to creep through me.

Then the door opened and a thin, angular-cheeked youth stepped inside. His eyes were dark and frightened, and he looked about timidly.

His survey reached me and lingered. "Are you Freddie Gage, the hoodlum preacher?" he asked. He seemed ready to bolt if the answer was negative.

"I am. What can I do for you?" I asked.

The boy gulped. "My name is Gerald, Reverend Gage, and I'm a junkie," he cried. "But I don't want to be a hophead anymore! Bat sent me. He said you think God can cure me."

The room was suddenly warm and cheery again. I stepped forward and put my arm around the boy's shoulder.

"I *know* God can cure you, son!" I boomed happily.

God did, too.

# 10
# Teen Liberators

"PULL ME OUT OF THE NET THAT
THEY HAVE LAID PRIVILY FOR ME:
FOR THOU ART MY STRENGTH."
—PSALM 31 :4

**O**vernight, the center became an exciting, busy doorway to redemption. Within a week, a dozen young men—young addicts—were sharing the third-floor dormitory with Gerald.

Out of the happy chaos that marked the first few days of operations, order gradually ensued. Seven young ministers, attending a Bible School, and two ministerial students joined the staff, although their salaries were paltry and their hours long.

I drew up a set of rules and regulations governing residents of the center. I realized that if the center were to fulfill its principal purpose to redeem the wrecked lives of these youngsters, strict discipline would have to be maintained.

I made it a condition of admission that anyone who was accepted had to agree to stay for at least 21 days. Anyone who left without permission before that period of time elapsed would not be permitted to return.

No tobacco, dope, beer, whiskey or liquor of any kind would be permitted on the premises. Daily Bible reading and chapel attendance was mandatory. No one was permitted to leave the grounds, day or night, without permission. If an applicant was employed, he was to go directly to his place of work from the center and return directly to the center upon completion of his workday.

All bags, boxes, parcels and clothes were inspected upon entering and leaving; and all mail, both incoming and outgoing, was subject to censorship. All residents were required to be neat and clean in dress, talk and manner at all times.

Reveille at the center would be at 6 A.M. each morning. Those residents whose physical condition permitted were required to share in a daily general cleanup of the center and of the grounds and in any other work that might arise.

Between 6 A.M. and 10 P.M.—lights out—the hours of the residents were rigorously regulated.

There were times for eating, times for playing, times for working, times for praying, times for study and times for conference. I had several copies of the regulations posted on all three floors of the center.

Then I went out and organized another gang!

This one was composed of young Christian men and women and we called ourselves Teen Liberators. The members of Teen Liberators were the "special forces" of the center, legionnaires of the Lord who witnessed and preached in taverns, pool halls, nightclubs, strip joints, and on the streets and in the alleys. I had a map of the city and county blown up, and on it I plotted the tough sections of Houston and of Harris County; and I pinpointed the known haunts and hangouts of junkies, hoodlums and teen-aged gangsters.

"Travel in groups of four to six," I instructed the Liberators. "And remember, you can't just go in and take over these places. You must use tact and diplomacy; and if the owners or managers object, you'll have to leave."

"What if someone tries to start a fight with us?" asked a young ministerial student.

"If you can't talk your way out of it, walk away," I

replied. "We never want to fight unless it's absolutely necessary to protect ourselves."

The adventures of the Liberators were many and varied.

The first group of hoodlums brought to the center en masse was ushered in by six triumphant girls.

"Where did you round them up?" I asked the squad leader. She gave me a bright smile. "Down on the waterfront," she chirped. "You know, that big bar down there!"

I knew. It was one of the most notorious dives in the South. Thereafter, girl Liberators were forbidden to work the waterfront.

One night I led a band of Liberators into a North Side hangout and asked the manager if we might "witness for Christ to these people."

He shrugged. "Go ahead, kid, but they're not going to listen."

He was almost correct. We moved from table to table, handing out newly printed brochures on the center and quoting Scripture. Our literature was wadded up and thrown on the floor, our Bible verses ignored.

There was a young girl sitting alone at one table. I began to witness to her; and when she seemed receptive, I sat down. Suddenly I was yanked to my feet. I found myself facing an angry young man.

"What in the hell are you trying to do, anyway?" he demanded in wolfish tones.

"I'm talking to her about Jesus," I replied, disengaging myself and stepping back.

The hood guffawed. "Jesus? Man, don't come on with that rib! You're trying to steal my girl." His hand slid in his pocket, and when it emerged, a bright blade flashed.

"I'm going to cut your head off!"

Several of those who had disdained us earlier leaped up and grabbed the man. "No, he's not ribbing, and he's not

163

trying to steal your hide. He's really a preacher. Cool it," one said.

Another stuck one of the brochures in the hood's face, straightening it. "There, see! That's his picture."

The hood glared at the crumpled brochure, and the scowl left his face. He pocketed his knife and grinned at me. "Okay, Parson, sit down. I'll argue religion with you!"

He lost the debate. I won him first to the center and then to Christ!

Other Liberators had to endure other trials. One of our young ministers entered a bar frequented by dope pushers, junkies and prostitutes and began witnessing to the patrons. A scantily-clad B-girl pushed him down into a chair and plopped her piquant curves onto his lap.

"Okay, baby, let's see how sincere you are," she cooed, cuddling up to him.

The minister was shocked, stunned and then tempted. But he recovered and, opening his Bible, began to read from the Psalms. The girl's arms loosened from about his neck and she slid off his lap, her face flushed with shame.

Two of those watching made decisions for Christ!

There was the night, too, when we invaded a pool hall and 17 youngsters accepted Christ and left with us. Jubilantly, we knelt in a huge circle on the parking lot and began giving thanks to God. The prayer session lengthened, and then lights bathed the parking lot.

"All right, you people, don't move!" a stern voice cracked. There were policemen all around us.

I looked up at a detective, lifting my Bible. "We were only praying."

His features contorted in surprise, and then they were laughing. "Praying! We thought you were shooting dice!"

Nickie came to the center.

We had been in need of a receptionist and housemother

since the opening of the center, but I had not been able to find a qualified person. One evening, I answered a knock on my office door and there was Nickie. She had short, brown hair and dark, pensive eyes. "Brother Gage, I want to volunteer."

Nickie was a joy and an inspiration and one of the most dedicated Christians with whom I have ever been associated. In the few months that she was with us, she not only performed the duties of a receptionist and housemother, but she shared the work load with all of us.

In her "spare time," Nickie kept a diary! I think some excerpts from her journal might serve to give an insight into the activities of the center and some of the problems that we encountered.

### NICKIE'S DIARY

January 1st: A mother called for us to talk to her son who is a drug addict. Two staff workers went to his home and brought him back to the center. The boy is hooked on H. He was in very bad shape.

January 4th: We had a board meeting attended by 31 ministers and laymen. All were inspired by the boys' testimony of what Christ has done for them here. . . .

January 5th: Associate Director Jerry Bernard spoke on juvenile delinquency at the Memorial Drive Baptist Church . . . boy came to the center who has been in prison for narcotics . . . he is living a messed-up life. . . . Teen Liberators working on the streets.

January 6th: Teen Liberators presented a program at Bellaire High School this morning. . . . Ladies from Melrose Baptist, Houston and Highlands Baptist and La Marque showered the center with gifts of food and many useful items. . . . Calls are coming in from all over the nation to the Teen Liberators headquarters for help for teen-agers in all kinds of trouble. . . .

January 7th: New boy checked into the center and accepted Christ as his personal Savior. . . . Evangelist Mickey Bonner taught the boys their Bible class today.

January 9th: Over 25 Teen Liberators invaders led by Freddie Gage are on the streets, taking the Gospel to gang hideouts today.

January 11th: New addict was brought to the center. He is very sick and is going through cold turkey. . . . One of the boys to court today. Case was dismissed.

January 15th: A father brought his boy all the way from Tulsa, Oklahoma, today. Boy is drug addict. Heart-breaking, as boy refuses to stay because of (center's) high standards. He's only 20 years old and already (has) spent four years behind bars. O, if God's people could only wake up to the need!

January 16: Two new boys checked into the center. Both drinking. Workers stayed up most of the night praying and working with the boys.

January 19th: Very busy day. People came from everywhere. Ministers, missionaries, policemen, attorneys . . . people from all walks of life. And mothers and fathers whose boys are in trouble . . .

January 20th: Calls are coming from schools, jails, churches, for boys to give testimony of what God is doing. Reverend Ray Hoekstra states "this is the greatest work of God I have ever seen . . ."

January 22nd: Boys close their first revival. Different boy in center preached each night—40 decisions for Christ were made.

February 2nd: Another boy checks into the center. Boy is only 15, has been to reform school.

February 3rd: Another boy checked into center seeking help. Freddie asked me, "What happened to the word 'concern?' "

February 7th: A girl addict accepted Christ. Also her husband, drug addict, accepted Christ. Young homosexual came seeking help . . . also a young lesbian.

February 8th: Calls again coming from everywhere. Youth in trouble; kids on glue . . . dope addicts . . . sex perverts. . . . How could you ever get Christians to believe it?

February 12th: Grandfather came to center . . . grandson going on trial today. Jerry and a minister go before the judge . . . boy is paroled to the center. Fine boy, 17 years old, saved from prison.

February 14th: Another addict comes to center. . . . Young prostitute here seeking help. . . . Letters and calls this month from 25 states, two foreign countries, in regard to Teen Liberators.

The ministry of the center was based on faith, and we trusted God to supply our needs from month to month. As the poet, William Cowper, wrote:

> God moves in a mysterious way
> His wonders to perform;
> He plants His footsteps in the sea
> And rides upon the storm.

Again and again, we saw demonstrated the mystic ways of God. Once, with 23 boys in residence, we found ourselves with a cupboard as bare as Old Mother Hubbard's. We had no money with which to buy staples, and very few of Houston's grocery stores extend credit. We called several without finding one that would allow us groceries on the cuff.

"Don't worry, the Lord will provide," Nickie smiled.

"Amen," I grinned.

A few minutes later, the front door opened, and a dozen or more colorfully dressed, pretty young ladies swept in—each of them burdened with bulky bags.

"Could you people use some food?" their leader asked

merrily. "We were supposed to deliver this to a party, but we're lost, and the party is, too—and we sure can't take this stuff back to the dorm!"

They were members of a college sorority. The bags contained enough bread, meat, canned goods and other staples to last us four days!

We were perpetually in debt, for the cost of operating the center expanded as our horizons broadened. We had monthly salaries to meet and the cost of operating two vehicles (both bought on a promise to pay "something" each month). There was the cost of school fees and allowances— not only bus fare, school supplies and school fees for boys attending Houston schools, but college aid to boys who had left the center to enroll in out-of-town Christian colleges. We had other promotional and educational expenses, too— Bibles and books, the cost of a monthly newsletter, brochures, tracts and the like. In addition, there was the cost of clothes, food, linens, soaps, towels, toilet articles and other necessities too numerous to mention.

The Lord always managed to bail us out just as the boat seemed certain to sink. At one time, with $6,000 in various liabilities facing the center, we hit upon a grandiose method to deliver us from debt. We staged a banquet! We rented one of the city's most pretentious club rooms, and I engaged one of the nation's foremost religious singers and sent out thousands of invitations at $3.50 each. Hundreds responded, and the banquet was held; but as I looked over the feasting hall, I knew that the net proceeds would not surpass $2,500.

Then, as we were preparing to leave, following the benediction, a quiet-faced man stopped me. "Brother Gage, I'd like to help," he said, handing me a check.

I thanked him and glanced at the check. Then I almost smothered him in gratitude. It was for $3,500!

I was continually amazed at the people who appeared at

the center to help, either with a financial contribution or to lend their services. There were Jews, there were Catholics, there were Quakers, there were Mormons and there were people of every other faith.

And there were people who professed no faith.

"I am not a believer, but I appreciate what you are trying to do here in the name of humanity," one man told me, after tendering a check for a generous amount. He may not be a believer, but I will never feel that he is an atheist.

A prominent socialite came to the center with a contribution, but stayed for services and made a decision for Christ!

We desperately needed a piano, but had to put off purchasing one until we could afford the expenditure. We never had to purchase the piano. A lady gave us one.

"It's not a good one, really," she said. "But it only needs about $100 worth of repairs to be an excellent piano."

A little later, the telephone rang and Nickie answered. She replaced the receiver with a smile. "That was a woman who is sending us $100 for our piano fund!"

There were tribulations. Teen Liberators were jeered, spat upon, reviled, cursed and, at times, threatened with bodily harm or death. Once, witnessing in a notorious sin den, a young hoodlum, high on pills, actually attacked me with a knife. I disarmed him, but I could not convert him.

We were, however, proving the theory behind Teen Liberators. No one could deny the results. No dope habit, or any other form of addiction for that matter, was proof against the power of God!

At this writing, I could give over 200 examples of young men who were once trapped like insects in the spider web of dope addiction or alcoholism, but who are now leading victorious lives.

Joe is one of them. He is typical of the more hardened criminals with which we are coping, although Joe is no longer either hardened or criminal. He has been born again in Christ. Listen to excerpts from his life story, as he recorded it for our use:

I was raised in the San Felipe Courts, near downtown Houston. In a family of six boys and one girl, I was the second to the oldest child. I was a thief from the time I was five, and by the time I was 13 I was smoking weed. I started using goof balls when I was 14.

I never took anything serious in my life until I was 18. Then I heard a judge sentence me to two years in the Texas State Penitentiary. That was serious.

In my early teens, I snatched women's purses, committed burglaries and robbed a few homes. But when I was in the ninth grade at school, I started selling weed. After that I didn't have to steal or rob anymore. Business was always good and I never had to worry about money. . . .

I always wanted to be somebody in this world, and I knew it took money to go first class. When I was 15, I bought my first pair of $21.00 shoes. The older fellows that I admired all wore those high-priced shoes, and I so desperately wanted to be admired by the older guys. They dressed sharp and had fine-dressed women. They stayed high on dope most of the time, had large rolls of money and never had to work.

These ways of the underworld became my goal in life. . . . When I was 18, I got caught with a half pound of weed and a pistol. The pistol was stolen. Sure enough, they put a high hand on me. . . . In prison, I got hardened up a little more. . . . I was discharged after 14 months. . . . My brother and my father picked me up. We took my father home, and then my brother and I proceeded to make up for lost time . . . I went right back to the weed and then to the "Stuff," heroin. . . . I was doing exactly as I pleased." One morning I woke up . . . (and) realized I was hooked. I had become addicted to heroin. . . . I was on it for 10 years. . . . I have been in and out of jails, but that didn't break the habit. . . . I was living in sin and crime. . . . I would do most anything for score money. . . . I wanted to die.

Then one night, a few months ago, Bobby M. and I got to talking about how we needed to pull up for a while and get straight. Bobby M. had heard about this place, called Teen Liberators, run by an ex-hood. . . .

Bobby M., a high school sports star, recited a similar story. So did Joe V., known as "Sleepy Brother."

Not all those who passed through Teen Liberators were dope addicts. Vernon was a gang leader called to our attention by probation authorities. Mike was a drunkard. H.C. was a thief. Tommy was a school dropout turned away by his family because he fathered an illegitimate child. Denny was a homeless youth we found sleeping in a bus station. Pat was a glue sniffer. Bill was a pillhead.

Where are they now? Bobby and Joe are students in an East Texas college, studying for the ministry. Joe is now a warehouse worker. Vernon and Tommy are now students at a Bible school. Mike is in the United States Air Force. H.C., Denny and Bill all have good jobs. Pat is back in high school. All of them, and dozens of others, are now dedicated Teen Liberators, witnessing on the streets, in the bars, in the pool halls, on the street corners and in Houston's poverty-stricken areas to the glory and power of God.

Early in 1965, Teen Liberators established a rapport with Harris County's criminal judges, juvenile judges and probation officials and with the Texas Youth Council; and many youths who otherwise were distined to go to prison or to reform school are instead on parole to Teen Liberators.

Not every youngster who came to the center seeking help could be accommodated, of course. There simply was not room. To meet the needs of these troubled youngsters, Teen Liberators initiated an "out-patient" program, counseling with such boys at the center or in their homes and keeping in close contact with them until their belief in the Lord was strong enough to meet the challenges and temptations of the world.

On the theory that it is better to build boys than to mend men, we carried the Teen Liberators' program into the junior and senior high schools and before civic groups and business groups.

My one regret was that the center could not lodge and cater to female addicts and delinquent girls, but state laws and common sense prohibited the mingling of the sexes. Those girls who came to the center seeking help, or whom we sought out on the streets or in bars, were ministered to on an out-clinic basis. While the number of girls won to Christ and cured of dope addiction totaled far less than the number of men, we nonetheless could chalk up dozens of distaff victories.

One incident involving a young girl still saddens me whenever it comes to mind. She had applied at the center for help and was receiving counseling and financial aid, but the burning demands for drugs made by her flesh prevailed over her mind. Somewhere, one night, she made a connection and then overfixed.

She was near death when someone—never identified—found her and called police. The officers who investigated found our literature in her purse and called Teen Liberators to tell us the name of the hospital to which she had been admitted.

Bobby and four other boys from the center went to the hospital to see her and pray for her, but she died without regaining consciousness.

I was out of the city at the time. Bobby told me of the aftermath.

"I went over to the funeral home, after she was laid out in her casket, to pay my respects, although I had not known her," Bobby said. I looked at the register on the table next to her casket, and no one had been to see her. The next morning, several of us returned for the funeral. My name was still the only one on the register! She had died alone, and had it not been for us, a group of strangers, she would have gone to her grave alone!

I still wonder how many girls like her will go to their graves alone before the churches of America fully awaken to the frightening national problem of our wayward girls?

Time passed, and one day I received one of those still familiar calls. It was from a friend of Jug Silvers.

"Cat, Jug was gunned down tonight in a bar," said the friend. "His wife said he wanted you to preach his funeral."

I did.

I returned from his funeral in a somber mood, for it had been my hope that someday I could lead Jug to Christ. In the months before his death, he had seemed receptive and had even promised to visit the center.

"You stick with it and go all the way, kid," Jug commented gruffly. "Me? I dunno. And it really doesn't matter. Me changing my life wouldn't make a bit of difference in the scales of humanity, anyway."

Jug never came by Teen Liberators. And I was never able to show him the error of his words. For he was wrong.

When you change one life, you change the world.

# Epilogue

There is no end, as such, to this story. New chapters are being written daily in the old house on Austin Street. While we can point to the Christian efforts of Teen Liberators and say, "This method works—God rehabilitates," we have, however, made but small inroads into the dark forests of the underworld and the world of restless and troubled youth.

There are many addicts and troubled youths still on the streets of Houston. The slums and blighted areas of the city are still fertile ground for the flowering of crime, pornography, perversion and corruption. Multiply the streets and slums of Houston by the number of other cities with similar problems in America, and you will have the larger canvas of crime with which we as a nation are concerned.

Teen Liberators is winning increasing support from law enforcement agencies, judges, doctors, sociologists and educational and civic groups who, together with a growing number of churches, recognize the value of a Christian rehabilitation center as a vital force in the fight to stem the alarming increase in crime and delinquency in today's society.

So, with faith in God, we are broadening the horizons of Teen Liberators.

Presently being worked out are plans for Liberators Institute For Training (LIFT), which will prepare poorly educated boys to hold a job. The purpose of LIFT will be to teach a trade to those who are reached through Teen Liberators, to train them in living a Christian life on the job, to prepare them to meet the challenges and temptations of the world with a faith that overcomes and to assist such youngsters financially by providing job opportunities after sufficient training.

At this writing, Teen Liberators has acquired a 20-acre tract near League City, south of Houston on the Gulf Freeway, on which stands a large Spanish-type villa and several lesser buildings. It is a boy's paradise, and it is on this acreage that a new Teen Liberators center will be built. It is hoped that facilities for both boys and girls will be provided, including a gymnasium, training center, dormitories and individual cottages. It is hoped the center will eventually accommodate 1,000 youngsters!

The old house in Austin is still in use as a "command post," and Teen Liberator "recruiting centers" are being established in other parts of Houston.

Much thought is being given, too, to Teen Liberators centers in Dallas, San Antonio, Fort Worth, Atlanta, New Orleans, Detroit, Chicago, Kansas City and other metropolitan cities.

Ambitious undertakings? Certainly—but we are determined to proceed, convinced that, with God's help, all things are possible.

And Jesus Christ is chairman of the board of Teen Liberators.

# Appendix

## THE TEEN LIBERATOR MESSAGE TO DRUG
## ADDICTS AND ALCOHOLICS

There is a cure for drug addiction and alcoholism. It doesn't matter how long a person has been addicted—he or she can be cured. Here are the five steps to that cure.

### 1. ADMIT YOU ARE HOOKED!

It doesn't matter whether you take off (fix) once a day or 10 times a day, you are hooked. So why not admit it?

Quit talking about a big habit or a little habit. A habit is a habit. You're either hooked or you're not hooked; you're either an alcoholic or you're not, so be honest. If you don't think you're hooked now, wait—it won't be long.

Quit trying to cut down your habit. You can't do it. You know you can't help yourself, so why do you keep trying? No one can help you if you just want to control your habit or shoot it up on weekends. There is no such thing as a controlled habit. You will shoot all the hope you can get and you know it! You will drink all the booze you can get your hands on!

Admit to yourself, "I'm a drug addict! I'm hooked!" or, "I'm an alcoholic. I can't help myself." Then you are ready for the next step.

## 2. QUIT LOOKING FOR AN EASY WAY OUT!

There is no simple, magic cure. There are no synthetic drugs or substances that can pull you out. Hospitals can't help you on a permanent basis. Just ask anyone who has been there. You're out of the hospital and right back on the spike! You can go back to the hospital 100 times, but you would still be the same—hooked! A clinic can't help you either, and deep in your heart you know it. Maybe you won't admit it, but it's true. How many times have you been to a clinic already? And you've gone right back on the needle every time.

No doctor, psychiatrist or hypnotist can cure you. A doctor can pacify you with some pills. A psychiatrist can tell you why you're an addict, but he can't cure you. Posthypnotic suggestion can't combat a strung-out habit.

Seminars and group therapy programs do not produce permanent cures, in spite of all the claims. Homes for addicts that practice seminar sessions cannot put in you what it takes to stay clean when you are on your own and in a real crisis.

Cold turkey is the best and quickest way to start a cure. Throwing away the bottle is the only way to stop drinking. Cutting down on your supply with medication is just an excuse to prolong your habit. Cold turkey never killed anyone. It's that way in jail. It's the best way.

You must quit smoking. No addict can be permanently cured until he is off cigarettes for good. If you can't quit your little habits, how are you going to quit your big habits? Furfural is a toxin in tobacco that will drive you back to the needle. What's the difference if you're addicted to tobacco or drugs? They are both habits of the mind. I dare anyone in the world to prove to me that an addict is cured if he is still smoking!

Don't ask for help just to please someone else. You are only fooling yourself if you look for help just to keep a wife, mother or friend happy. You've got to want to help yourself!

You can't be cured in three weeks or three months. So forget about a job and your future for about a year. You have to get away from your so-called friends and from your connections—out of the city, out of the community, out of the streets. For at least one full year! You don't need a job right now—you couldn't keep it anyway.

Don't expect to be trusted or babied. You can't fool experienced people in the field of narcotics, so quit working angles. You may be sick, but you're not a little baby. If you can run around looking for connections, you can work for a cure.

### 3. GIVE YOURSELF TO GOD!

God is the only one who can cure you. Nothing is impossible with God! If anyone claims cures outside the power of God, they are lying.

You must believe that the Bible is the Word of God and that it has secrets to your cure. "You shall know the truth and the truth shall make you free."

It is not enough to just believe in God. You must believe in His Son, Jesus Christ. The Bible makes this promise to you: If you will confess Him as your Savior, He will make you into a new man. The old life will pass away, and everything will become new. You will become a new creature.

Open up your heart to God even more than you would to a psychiatrist and tell Him all about your problems. Then confess to Jesus all your sins and every bad thing that you can remember you have done. Ask Him to forgive your sins and to come into your heart. He will drive out the desire for drugs and give you power over it!

Don't just think prayers to God—talk out loud to Him. He understands you and knows all about your sins and problems, but He wants you to talk to Him. While you are talking out loud to God, you will suddenly know what prayer really is.

Talk to God at least five times a day. Read the Bible every day and fill your mind with thoughts from its verses. Keep asking for His help, even if you have to do it a thousand times a day. He will never get tired of listening.

You must have faith in God! When you connect with a pusher, how do you know he isn't giving you rat poison instead of H? You shoot it up without testing it under a microscope because you had faith it was junk. If you can trust a dope pusher, why can't you trust God? *He never lets you down!*

### 4. START PLANNING YOUR LIFE
### ALL OVER AGAIN!

The moment you surrender your life over to God, that is the time to start planning all over again. Think back to the time before you started using drugs—or drinking alcohol. What was your ambition? Find what you want to do, then start making plans.

All of your plans must start with God. Make Him your partner and don't ever let Him leave your life.

Don't make Him leave you by your neglect. Give God first chance to use your life. Maybe He will want you to help other addicts when you are fully cured.

You can never be around your old neighborhood or your old friends. Stay away from your old life as if it were hell itself. Stay away from your old hangouts, instead of testing yourself to see if you are cured—that would be tempting God. Find new friends and brothers who are clean.

If you have no plans for your life and you are sure you can't help others, then mark down on a piece of paper five things that you think you would like to do or be. Spend a few weeks investigating what is involved in all of these five things—then choose the one which appeals to you most. You must choose a goal! You can never again be a loafer. You can never again be a floater without ambition. *Know what you want to do— then go after it!* Indecision will ruin you.

You must learn to love the things you once hated and learn to hate the things you once loved. You can do the right things now because God gives you the power to do them.

### 5. SHAKE OFF ALL YOUR OLD FEARS!

Fear is the demon that turned you into a drug addict to begin with. When you turn your life over to God, you never have to fear again. When Jesus comes to live in your heart, He drives away all fears and doubts.

Don't be afraid that you will go back to the needle or the bottle. God guarantees a 100 percent cure. As long as you stay with God, He will stay with you. If you forsake God, you will go back to being an addict or an alcoholic. When Jesus comes to be with you, you need never fear.

Don't be afraid of your past. When God forgives

your sins, He forgets them. He will not hold them against you, and He will make society forget them, too. Make restitution when you can, but when you can't, leave it all in God's hands.

Don't ever be afraid that God will drop you. He has never done that, and He even promises to send an angel to watch over you in all your ways.

Don't ever be afraid of what people will say or think. Keep your eyes on Jesus, and you will never be disappointed or confused.

When fear starts coming into your mind to confuse and bother you, when you start getting restless, get away by yourself and kneel before God. Ask Him to keep you in perfect peace. *He Will Keep You From All Your Fears!*